BUYING REAL ESTATE FOR PENNIES <u>ON THE</u> DOLLAR

BUYING REAL ESTATE FOR PENNIES ON THE DOLLAR

ANDREW JAMES McLEAN

CONTEMPORARY
BOOKS

CHICAGO

Library of Congress Cataloging-in-Publication Data

McLean, Andrew James.
    Buying real estate for pennies on the dollar : how to make a
fortune in foreclosures / Andrew J. McLean.
        p.   cm.
    Includes index.
    ISBN 0-8092-3944-2 (pbk.)
    1. Real estate investment.   2. Foreclosure.   3. Tax sales.
I. Title.
HD1382.5.M316   1992
332.63'24—dc20   92-8600
                                                               CIP

The comments and recommendations in this book are the opinions of the author and are based on his extensive research and twenty-four years of experience in the real estate business. Every realty transaction is unique, change is inevitable in the world of real estate, and relevant laws and regulations will probably change after this book is printed. Therefore, if expert assistance is required when making investments, the reader should seek the advice of a competent professional person.

To Bob and Barbara Durling

Contents

Preface

The greatest banking crisis since the Great Depression has resulted in a massive volume of foreclosed property coming on the market. *Buying Real Estate for Pennies on the Dollar* is intended to be a thorough and informative step-by-step guide to profitable investment in foreclosed residential housing—specifically, single-family houses to 20-unit buildings—including how to renovate and profitably rent or sell your acquired units.

Within the book you'll also read about some of my personal experiences investing in several houses and small apartment buildings. You'll read what to look for in a foreclosed property, how to evaluate it, how to buy it during any one of the three phases of foreclosure—default, the foreclosure sale, and the real estate owned phase (when the lender owns the property)—and how to renovate it. You'll learn how to buy at auctions and tax sales, and how to implement a variety of proven money-making ideas and strategies. Featured are specific guidelines on what to look for and what to avoid when investing in a distressed property. These guidelines will act as your blueprint for profitable real estate investment.

We'll begin with how real estate values took such a dive and the reason the market today is so glutted with foreclosed property. After that you'll discover specific guidelines of exactly what to look for in a profitable realty investment. From there you'll learn about where to find property and what to do with it after you own it, including profitable improvements that will add thousands to the value of your property. Included are powerful investment strategies, designed for both first-time home buyers and real estate professionals, that allow you to profit dramatically in today's real estate market.

I'm convinced that one or more of these instructional tools can provide just the information and inspiration you need to help achieve your investment goals. By learning to use these tactics in conjunction with a well-conceived plan, then properly implementing everything you've learned, you can achieve whatever goals you aspire to.

Within the contents of this book you'll learn:

- How to buy auction-eligible properties and other real estate for pennies on the dollar
- How to buy at tax sales
- How to invest during any one of the three phases during which foreclosure property may be available
- What to look for in a property
- Where to find your "diamond in the rough"
- How to make quick and accurate appraisals
- How to make profitable renovations and improvements
- Profitable strategies and powerful money-making ideas

All you need is the desire, the skill, and the perseverance to profit at real estate investing. I, of course, cannot supply the desire and perseverance. But I can enhance your skills by showing you principles and tactics to adhere to.

Besides spelling out key guidelines for evaluating the properties available and choosing the one that best suits your needs, this book will continue to assist you as a handbook throughout your investment career.

If you've never purchased real estate before, or if you own a home but are considering buying other real estate as an investment, *Buying Real Estate for Pennies on the Dollar* provides sound advice on how to do it, and do it profitably.

Best of luck and good investing.

Acknowledgments

My thanks to Mike Snyder of Americana Realty for his editorial assistance as well as his expertise in helping me to negotiate the purchase of the Nevada properties.

~ 1 ~

Introduction

Could I interest you in a cozy beachfront home in southern California for $39,000? How about a nineteen-unit apartment building near downtown Los Angeles for $110,000? Perhaps you desire a deluxe two-bedroom condominium fronting the eighteenth hole on a golf course in Phoenix for $49,000. Or have you ever thought about owning a small ranch—zoned for horses, of course—on a half acre of land overlooking the Las Vegas strip for $75,000? Or might you be interested in retiring to a beachfront penthouse overlooking Miami Beach for $59,000.

These are just a few tantalizing samples of the distressed properties available through bank foreclosures, public auctions, the Resolution Trust Corporation (RTC), and other government agencies. On the surface, some of these bargain-priced properties seem too good to be true. And in some cases they are. But many are great buys if you're prepared to renovate them and, more importantly, to buy the right property at the right price!

Of course, no one is going to hand you the excellent ones on a silver platter. And no one will tell you up front that the plumbing is missing in six units of that nineteen-unit building in Los Angeles. Or that in the Miami Beach condo, all the windows are smashed, not to mention that the bathtubs and sinks have been ripped from their fittings.

Regardless of the problems some of these properties have, there's still plenty of money to be made by shrewd investors who know the techniques for profitable investing. And when you read the rest of this book, you'll learn those techniques, along with how to find the right property and buy it for pennies on the dollar. You'll also learn how to renovate that property, then rent or sell it in the not-so-distant future.

You begin with clearly established objectives—the purchase of a first or second home, for example—then implement the blueprint for investment offered here. Along the path to success, your confidence will be enhanced by the education and experience you gain. Reading about distressed property, combined with the actual experience of investing and getting involved in real estate, raises your levels of skill and confidence to a point where your chances of achieving success are excellent.

WHY INVEST IN FORECLOSED RESIDENTIAL REAL ESTATE?

Generally speaking, you need real estate. You not only need a home to live in, you also need shelter from excessive income taxes and a hedge against the eroding effects of inflation on your hard-earned income. If you aspire to achieve your dreams, as most of us do, you need additional income and a sound investment vehicle in order to develop financial security for you and your family. Investing in real estate offers you all this, plus tax shelters unavailable with other common forms of investment. More importantly, it offers you control over your own investment destiny. You don't need third-party advisers, such as stockbrokers or financial consultants whose judgment might be unsound, to make investments for you in volatile markets where you have no control.

Reasons for Investing in Residential Real Estate

The most common reasons for investing in residential real estate are to earn a quick profit, to generate income, and to own a home of one's own. When I started, I wanted a home, knowing that eventually it would earn income when I rented it and a profit when I sold it.

My reasons for investing kind of blossomed after buying my first home. I was initially inspired to buy it when I had to preserve $5,500, the amount I had left from an initial inheritance of $11,000. While a student at Michigan State University, I fixed the place up and rented it out. Then I bought a second house, knowing that five of the six bedrooms could be rented to other students while I lived there.

My own investment experience is with single-family houses and small apartment buildings. If you're a first-time investor, consider all the options. But keep in mind that the emphasis in this book is on becoming a specialist in the profitable buying and selling of single-family houses and small apartment buildings of up to twenty units.

Quick Profit

Buy low, sell high, and when you do it, the shorter the turnover time, the better. You can earn phenomenal profits if—and that's a big *if*—the marketplace is strong and everything goes exactly as planned. I would advise this strategy only if you are an experienced investor with strong cash reserves. That's because you'll need cash to carry you during the holding period. If resale of the property is delayed, holding costs erode the anticipated profit, especially if the property remains vacant.

Income

Imagine the following scenario. You buy a house, move into it, renovate it, then a few years later sell it, and with part of the profits buy another. Or you could, instead of selling it, rent it to tenants and buy another house with your savings. This way you own two houses while living in one of them. You'll earn steady rental income while at the same time enjoying other benefits, like tax-deductible expenses and depreciation allowances that shelter your salary income.

Home Ownership

If you are considering a property to serve as your principal residence as well as an investment, you'll have the potential to enjoy the many advantages of investing your money in a home. Perhaps the greatest advantage is the potential for the value of your property to appreciate. Also, the government provides tax deductions for homeowners. Building up equity as you pay your mortgage is a form of forced savings. When you sell or trade your home, you can defer paying taxes on the gain in its value (the capital gain). You also have control over your investment in a marketplace that traditionally has been stable (compared to the stock or commodity markets). Finally, of course, there's the noneconomic benefit of the satisfaction of owning your own home without the hassles of a landlord.

Reasons for Investing in Foreclosed Real Estate

Although the decline in the real estate market and the glut of foreclosed properties constitute a crisis for both the banking industry and Uncle Sam, it's a virtual gold mine of opportunity for shrewd investors. Why? Because you can buy distressed property for pennies on the dollar with very good terms. And these golden opportunities will likely be available for at least a decade to come.

There are no restrictions whatsoever as to who can purchase distressed realty. No special license is required. You don't have to be a licensed real estate broker or salesperson as long as you're investing for your own account. You don't even have to be a citizen of the United States to purchase property in foreclosure. Information regarding distressed property is a matter of public record without reserve to anyone.

IS THIS STRATEGY FOR YOU?

Real estate investing is not for everyone. To succeed in most professions, you have to like, at least a little, what you're doing, and this axiom is especially true about investing in distressed property. Before you get started, seriously ask yourself, "Is this what I really want?" Do you have the willingness or desire to take the time to fix things up? At least a little desire, anyway? And, if you intend to later rent the property, are you prepared to be a landlord, to be active in the overall management of your property?

Remember that distressed property is purchased as-is, without warranties. Most foreclosed properties have spent months, perhaps years, boarded up and neglected. Real estate, particularly the improvements built upon the land, needs proper attention, care, and maintenance to sustain its optimum value.

Much of the profit gained in buying and selling distressed property is earned by owners doing most of the renovation labor themselves. When the investor must pay contractors to work on the property, the costs go up, shrinking the profit potential. Thus, it helps if you're a skilled tradesperson such as a carpenter, plumber, bricklayer, or electrician. Other occupations with helpful skills include being a draftsman, painter, carpet installer, or interior designer. All these skills are extremely useful in owning residential real estate.

Much of my own experience at managing apartments came from being employed by R&B Development, which owned twenty-eight thousand apartment units nationwide. From this experience I felt comfortable when I bought my first apartment building, knowing that I had the skills to profitably manage it.

A Word of Caution

Bear in mind that property can become distressed and eventually end up being foreclosed on for several reasons. The most common causes frequently arise from the deterioration of the neighborhood, financial difficulty, and poor management (inability to rent a unit).

As a result, foreclosed property is seldom in habitable condition. It is, of course, sold as-is, without the seller making any warranties or promises to repair it. It is your responsibility to determine whether or not the property is a worthwhile investment.

Most inexperienced investors of foreclosed property overlook one very important fact: *what you see is not often what you get.* More than likely, the property you're evaluating has been neglected over the past few years. When property owners begin getting into financial trouble, the first thing they neglect is building maintenance. The last thing they overlook are the mortgage payments on the building. Thus, you can expect at least two years of neglected maintenance on the typical foreclosed property. Because the property was left unattended for such a period, you might even find that robbers have gutted it of all plumbing fixtures or that many of its operational systems do not function properly.

But all these negatives really don't matter if you allow for them. You can still make plenty of money on some of these distressed properties. You just need to know what to look for (as well as what to avoid), and how to buy and renovate the properties at the right price.

What It Takes from You

Besides the general goal of making big profits, first determine your objective for investing in real estate. For example, do you want to buy a home of your own to live in, to rent out, or to quickly resell for a profit?

Once you have specified your purpose for investing in a distressed property, you have to focus in on the type of property to buy. You say, "That's easy. I want a home of my own." But specifically what kind of home do you desire? Do you want a condominium, a mobile home, an apartment in a four- or six-unit apartment house, or a single-family house? Here's where you can begin to specialize. And, of course, a specialist is someone who is very good at what he or she does.

Before you decide on what type of property is best for you, you must consider many factors. Even the most careful evaluation of the numbers won't guarantee a profitable deal. You must first look at your own capabilities and experience. Consider the following important factors:

Do You Like What You're Doing?
Does the idea of buying a house in disrepair, moving in, renovating it, and later selling it for a $30,000 profit turn you on? Or what about the idea of moving into a four- or six-unit apartment house, renovating it, and being the live-in landlord?

For me, the motivation was twofold. I wanted a place of my own, and I saw a good way to earn a profit doing it. Making money in real estate meant financial independence. I realized early in life that if I continued working at my job, while at the same time investing my savings periodically in houses on a part-time basis, eventually I could quit my job and become a full-time investor.

How Much Time Do You Have?

You must consider how much time you have to give to your investment. For example, let's say you plan to refurbish a run-down singe-family house and later sell it or rent it out. The question of time will depend on whether or not you live in the house. It would take much more time if you were refurbishing a house and living somewhere else.

On the other hand, owning vacant land might be considered less demanding of your time. Some might think that all you have to do is sit around and watch it appreciate. But what if that piece of land must be rezoned to reach its optimum value? Then you'll have to spend many hours at planning board meetings, not to mention paying for engineering surveys and incidental legal costs.

Likewise, owning an apartment building when you have a competent live-in resident manager is a piece of cake. Then the absentee owner can virtually manage over the phone. But what about the time you'll need to get the building into habitable condition, not to mention the job of hiring a competent manager?

How Much Money Do You Need?

Theoretically, you could buy distressed property using several no-money-down concepts, where you borrow all the down payment and renovation capital. There was a time, especially during the hyperinflationary years of the mid-1970s to the early 1980s, when real estate values skyrocketed over short periods and high leverage (borrowing a large share of the purchase price) led to big profits. However, changes in the marketplace, such as slower rates of appreciation and less favorable tax shelter benefits, along with more stringent lending practices, promote a more conservative strategy. In the 1990s, positive cash flow is more important to the realty investor than maximum leverage.

HOW SMALL INVESTORS GET BIG

There are two types of investors, big and small. Except in the rare instance of a windfall inheritance, the big investor has gotten big by first making small investments, accumulating wealth, and then turning to bigger and better things—like owning huge apartment buildings and shopping centers.

Dr. Jerry Buss, owner of the Los Angeles Lakers and the Great Western Forum, started with a meager $1,000. With that modest investment, he bought one house, then another and another, and in time owned seven hundred houses. Eventually he parlayed those investments into the multimillion-dollar Los Angeles Lakers and Great Western Forum.

THE PLAN IN A NUTSHELL

Have you ever wondered why some people achieve financial prosperity and others do not? There are two primary reasons: the prosperous ones *are clear about their objectives* and *know the strategies for achieving their objectives*. The purpose of this book is to reveal powerful investment strategies that build on these tactics and turn your dreams into realities. You must supply the objectives, the commitment, and the proper implementation of the proven strategies offered.

This book shows you how to make money by investing in

residential real estate. What you'll be doing has been done for centuries. Buy low, sell high, and make a profit on the spread between the selling price and the acquisition cost (less, of course, the renovation cost). The less you pay to buy and renovate the property, the bigger your profit. If you spend excessively on renovations, your profit margin shrinks and so does your net profit.

Property in distress offers a great opportunity for almost anyone to earn investment profits. Most people can even invest in it in their spare time. In the beginning you have to be especially wary of some of the inherent pitfalls, but once you've acquired experience and confidence, you'll learn to avoid most of them. Meanwhile, I will offer you specific guidelines for exactly what to look for and what to avoid in a realty investment. You'll also read about proven money-making techniques and strategies that will show you how to profit from your investment.

Basically, you will be doing what millions of merchants have done for centuries: purchasing an item wholesale, packaging it, then earning a profit when it's sold at retail. This is, of course, an oversimplification, but it's true. More precisely, you'll be making a good buy on a distressed house, adding value by renovating it, then using several profitable techniques to earn income from it. The money you earn from this property is then reinvested in a second property as you continue to buy other distressed houses, sometimes moving in, then renovating and renting or selling them.

The Name of the Game Is Conversion

When you purchase a distressed fixer-upper and renovate it, you can use it first as a residence. Then, when you rent or sell it after buying another, the property becomes a profit maker. Converting a run-down fixer-upper into a beautiful, desirable home not only can give you a great feeling of satisfaction, it can be very profitable as well. Using the techniques featured in this book over an extended period of time, you can eventually achieve the ultimate goal of financial independence.

Specialization Is the Key

We live in the age of specialization. To be a specialist at something, especially a masterful one, you have to concentrate your efforts in a selective field of endeavor. Just as a noted attorney specializes in certain kinds of law or a physician specializes in a single branch of medicine, so you must specialize in one type of investing.

If you practice within a select segment of the overall marketplace, you have a better chance of gaining expertise and being successful. Say, for instance, that you're motivated to own your home. Then be selective in choosing exactly what you want—for instance, a single-family house as opposed to a condominium or a mobile home.

But more than anything, you want to specialize because it not only simplifies your tasks, it reduces risk and makes you more adept within a special market. Eventually you'll become more efficient at what you do, avoiding many of the pitfalls that can trip up neophyte investors. By gaining experience, you learn to develop an eye for what's a bargain and what's terribly overpriced. With experience, you learn to develop a trained eye for value and relevant costs. Only those who know market value can accurately make an appraisal to determine what is underpriced, what has potential for renovation at moderate cost, and what can be resold at a profit.

Learn the Terminology

When you become familiar with the terms and procedures involved with foreclosure, you'll not only gain a certain amount of confidence, you'll also be able to perform as a learned individual. When you add to that the proven guidelines and tactics that are featured later in the book, you will become able to obtain worthwhile investments more efficiently and confidently. At the same time, you'll learn to avoid properties that lack profit potential.

FROM CONSIDERATION TO DECISION

Knowing what capabilities and resources you'll need should help you decide the type of property to invest in, the amount of time you're willing to expend on the venture, and the purpose of your venture (quick profit from sale, steady income, or a home of your own). But all these decisions are just preliminary to the big one, deciding to actually purchase a property. You cannot do that successfully until you have learned what to look for and what's a good deal.

It all boils down to knowing the competitive market value of whatever it is you're shopping for. You must know what makes a good deal good, then you have to know how to find a property with those characteristics. Finally, you must learn to use techniques that will make those properties profitable. The following chapters will reveal exactly how to accomplish that, along with an overview of what's available in foreclosed property.

~ 2 ~

Why So Much Distressed Property Is on the Market

What makes this such a great time to invest in distressed properties? You can buy low and buy selectively because many foreclosed properties are on the market. This is because the real estate cycle in most parts of the country has been on a downswing. At the same time, many lenders are overburdened with defaulted loans and must sell off the real estate securing those loans.

PERIODS OF PROSPERITY AND RECESSION

The market for real estate, like business activity in general, tends to follow a cyclical pattern. Periods of economic growth, called expansions, are followed by downturns in business activity, commonly termed recessions (or depressions, such as the Great Depression of 1929, when the decline is more alarming and severe). Real estate booms tend to occur somewhat after a period of general economic expansion.

With the stage set for a real estate boom, overall prices rise in response to increased demand. Relatively low interest rates spur more borrowing, so businesses make investments and consumers buy more goods and services. Likewise, builders and developers begin new projects to keep pace with demand.

The pace accelerates, and prices go higher and higher. Exchanges multiply, profits seem never-ending and increasingly larger, and speculating begins. Speculators buy real estate to resell it for a quick profit, not to hold it as a long-term investment. The extraordinary profits become newsworthy as anxious first-time buyers clamor to get into the market to share them. Sound concepts of value are swept aside, and income returns seem of little consequence as true tests of value. The pace of property transfer quickens further as sites and buildings are sold and resold, always at higher prices.

This activity eventually levels off and continues for a time at a somewhat reduced pace. Then something happens to curb demand. Often it's a major world event that triggers the downturn. In 1979 it was a glut in the supply of petroleum on world markets, which caused drastic price reductions and enormous employee layoffs within the oil industry. And although the economy showed signs of weakening in 1988, the trigger came in 1990: the invasion of Kuwait by Iraq, which inevitably resulted in the Gulf War.

Whatever the event may be, it causes alarm, and the market slows gradually to a halt. Then some nervous but heavily loaded speculators begin to unload. Soon after, others follow suit in a wild rush. Meanwhile, to complicate matters further, developments that were conceived during the early stages of the boom are now completed and gradually emerge on the market, and it becomes overbuilt. *The downturn in real estate is under way.*

As soon as the trend becomes generally noted, market demand dries up, for nobody will buy in a falling market. The situation goes from bad to worse as mortgage commitments come due and buildings remain unoccupied. Owners liquidate (sell off) their holdings, sometimes over months or years and at a substantial discount.

This scenario, briefly, is the story of a boom and its succeeding recession.

Historically, boom periods tend to last upwards of seven years, while periods of recession have about a two-year duration. When times are prosperous and a real estate boom is in progress, few believe that it ever will be followed by a collapse. Likewise, when a recession is in full swing, few realty owners can be convinced that it will ever end and that good times will eventually return. Most people decline to believe that values may ever recover to their former levels and that the recession will end.

FORECLOSURES IN RELATION
TO BUSINESS CYCLES

The aggregate supply of foreclosed property throughout the land is directly related to the prevailing economic conditions. During periods of economic prosperity—commonly associated with low unemployment, rising real estate values, and thriving business activity—the supply of foreclosed property is typically minimal. But during periods of recession, the opposite is true. Serious unemployment, little or no appreciation in real property values, and slow overall business activity all add up to one thing: an abundant supply of foreclosures.

Yet the recession that began in 1988 was different from the others. Special negative factors—factors that did not exist in past recessions and made this one more severe—contributed to the collapse of the real estate market and inevitably caused the current crisis in the banking industry. The result is a massive volume of foreclosures never before seen in the history of American business.

THE CRISIS IN THE BANKING INDUSTRY

The failure rate of savings and loan institutions has been unprecedented since the 1930s, and many banks have suffered as well. The government insurance fund that protects deposits in these institutions has been running out of money. What's behind this crisis in the banking industry? The answer is that a combination of several factors came together to bring about a meltdown during the 1980s. The result will be billions of dollars, perhaps even trillions, in losses over the next decade or so.

Before 1982 members of the thrift industry—savings and loan institutions (S&Ls) in particular—made only conservative long-term home loans. Regulations restricted them from making certain other types of high-risk loans. The home loans were the S&Ls' bread and butter, and the industry as a whole remained solvent. S&Ls functioned conservatively, taking in depositors' savings and efficiently earning a modest profit by lending these deposits to home buyers.

Deregulation

Then, during the Reagan Administration, the seeds that spawned the crisis were inadvertently sown. The mood in Washington was to get government off the backs of American business. In pursuit of this endeavor, legislators began thinking (with all good intentions, of course) that deregulating the thrift industry would stimulate business.

It all started rather innocently. S&Ls had been restricted by law as to how much interest they could pay depositors. Meanwhile, other banking institutions (commercial banks) were offering investment vehicles that paid higher rates of interest, and the thrifts could not compete. Therefore, in 1980 Congress raised the rate of interest thrifts could pay depositors.

But America was in the midst of a deep recession, and the thrift industry was struggling in spite of the relaxed requirements. S&Ls were still regulated as to where they could invest money on deposit (essentially in the traditionally safe yet relatively unprofitable home mortgages). Because they were unable to earn enough income from home mortgages to justify paying competitive interest rates on deposits, they inevitably began to crumble.

Congress responded in 1982 by enacting the Garn-St Germain Depository Institutions Act, which eased more regulations and allowed thrifts to lend money on a greater variety of projects, such as shopping centers and ski resorts. This meant that your neighborhood S&L could not only offer higher interest rates on deposits, it could also lend those deposits on potentially high-yield projects (which inevitably carry a high risk). With the restraints removed, the more daring thrift operators (including some with criminal aspirations) began venturing into new fields of opportunity.

But where was the risk? If these high-yield projects proved successful, the thrift earned a profit and remained solvent. If the projects failed and borrowers defaulted on their loans, the depositors were protected by federal insurance—up to $100,000 per account!

The Tax Reform Act of 1986

During the mid-1980s, solving the dilemma of the budget deficit was a primary concern of our country's legislators. To this end, in 1986 Congress passed the Tax Reform Act, sweeping legislation that changed the real estate investment strategy not only of the public at large, but of the overall banking industry as well. Back then, the intention of Congress was twofold: to simplify the tax code and to generate more tax revenue by plugging up the traditional loopholes in the tax code (taking away many of the perks that investment in real estate offered).

Inevitably, this extensive tax reform had a dramatic negative effect on market values, rents, income, and rates of return on most real estate investments. To compensate for the loss in tax incentives, the public at large and the bankers were forced to seek out higher-yielding investments, which, of course, meant making riskier investments. And if you take away many of the incentives of owning real property, naturally there will be much less demand for it. Therefore, after 1986 tax reform was the primary factor in the general demise of real estate values throughout America.

The Final Blow

The final blow came when the Federal Home Loan Bank Board, which regulated the S&L industry, minimized the capital requirements for individual thrifts. This meant that S&Ls had to keep very little of their assets in cash reserves. The balance of their assets was primarily in the form of mortgage loans, some more risky than the conservative pre-1982 unregulated norm. If these high-risk mortgages (which potentially earned bigger yields) proved successful, the S&L made big profits. If these mortgages disintegrated into uncollectible loans, the S&L might go bankrupt. But because the government insured savers' deposits through the Federal Savings and Loan Insurance Corporation, only that agency would really lose any money.

When defaulting borrowers caused S&Ls to crumble like fallen cookies and the FSLIC realized that it lacked sufficient funds to pay the bill, the results were a catastrophe! Bailing out the S&Ls shows signs of being the biggest rip-off in the history of American business. And do you know who the ultimate loser is? You're right if you said the *American tax-payer*.

Now the lenders and Uncle Sam are selling off the cata-strophic results—hundreds of billions in foreclosed assets of the failed thrifts.

WHAT'S AVAILABLE

From Individual Lenders

Before the current banking crisis, lenders who had taken back property through foreclosure were not exactly thrilled with the idea of selling it to the public. Although there was always a lot of public interest in the purchase of foreclosures and many potential buyers were constantly inquiring about them, very few were successful purchasers. Back then banks consid-ered the inquiries a nuisance and usually gave a standard reply: sorry, nothing available. When they did liquidate their holdings, they usually did so through established real estate brokers the bank had previously done business with, directly to known buyers, or even to friends.

Of course, those were the good old days when foreclosure inventories were minimal and lenders could be selective in who they sold to. This is not the case anymore. In fact, I have actually seen a notice on the window of a bank here in Naples, Florida, stating, "Foreclosure Property Available. Inquire Within."

Generally speaking, it's difficult to put a handle on exactly what an individual bank or S&L has available. Considering the magnitude of the banking crisis and the abundance of foreclo-sures nationwide, whatever you want, they most likely have.

Foreclosure inventory of an institutional lender is commonly termed "real estate owned" (REO). If you're interested in purchasing REO, approach the REO department in person and meet its manager. Be specific about what it is you want (such as a single-family home or a fourplex). Establishing a personal relationship is the best way of getting into the REO business. More information about how to invest in REO is available in Chapter 5.

From Uncle Sam's Inventory

The property owned by the S&Ls being bailed out is sold by the federal Resolution Trust Corporation (RTC). Uncle Sam's daily expanding inventory of properties includes oil and gas fields, time-share apartments, half-finished condominium developments, mobile homes, hotels, commercial warehouses, land, athletic clubs, single-family houses (including some with all plumbing fixtures removed), vacation cottages, duplexes, ranches, and retirement homes. Despite the variety of bailout property available, more than 80 percent of the inventory listed in the first RTC publication, in the spring of 1990, was residential.

At that time thirty thousand properties were listed. Within six months, another half-million properties came on the market. And if that figure doesn't startle you, the most recent estimates predict about three million more properties will become available when the RTC takes a tally of the institutions that are now on the brink of faltering.

Among this massive volume of available bailout inventory are, of course, the properties classed under the headings "The Excellent! The Good! The Bad! And the Downright Ugly!" And you cannot always distinguish them without doing some necessary research. I'll show you how to accomplish this task, but first you should understand how Uncle Sam plans to dispose of this inventory.

How the RTC Works

In August 1989 the Financial Institutions Reform, Recovery and Enforcement Act (FIRREA) was signed into law. This law created the RTC and made it responsible for selling off the assets of the failed S&Ls. As of this writing, the RTC has established fifteen regional sales centers nationwide to coordinate marketing of its holdings.

At the outset of sales activity in January 1990, the RTC offered its first publication of available property to anxious would-be buyers. In a notice accompanying this 3,000-page book of listings, titled *Real Estate Asset Inventory,* the RTC made it clear that it would sell no property for less than 95 percent of its appraised value.

But you might say, "I'm a bargain hunter interested in buying foreclosed property at pennies on the dollar, not a meager five-penny discount!" And you're absolutely right. So were the countless other savvy investors who knew that the numbers and policies of the RTC had to change. Most of these potential buyers suspected that appraisals would be revised (because appraised value represents an educated estimate) or policy changed when the properties didn't sell within a few months.

Changes in Policy

So savvy investors held their ground, patiently waiting for a better opportunity. Then, almost five months later, the RTC announced that it would no longer maintain the minimum price of 95 percent of appraised value. Directors voted unanimously to allow regional managers to reduce the allowed selling prices on the properties it had for sale. Managers could accept purchase prices of up to 15 percent below appraised value on all properties that had been on the market at least four months. They also were allowed to reduce the minimum acceptable sales price another 5 percent if they did not sell within three months of the first price reduction.

That's 20 percent off appraised value, which is more in line with a bargain hunter's attitude of buying for pennies on the dollar. Shrewd investors who have the patience to keep an eye on specific properties will likely benefit the most. So do not allow deviations in RTC policy to impair your ambitions. Change can pay off handsomely if you anticipate it and prepare for it.

Two more instances of significant changes in RTC policy have also occurred. At the outset of sales activity, the agency announced: (1) that properties would be sold only through conventional channels using licensed real estate brokers, and (2) that no seller financing would be available to the general public. Within a year, both these rules were changed.

The rule stating that all properties would be sold only through conventional channels changed in May 1990. The RTC announced that it planned to sell $300 million of inventory at its first auction, scheduled for July. Furthermore, the Bush Administration supported further easing of RTC policy that would allow auctioned property to be sold at 30 percent below the appraised values.

The policy that no seller financing would be available has been reversed. Now seller financing is provided to the general public, and the minimum down payment has been reduced as well. When the policy was first changed to allow seller financing, the RTC required a minimum 25 percent down payment. Now the minimum is just 15 percent down.

As these changes suggest, any numbers and policies referred to in this book are apt to change as the bailout bureaucracy evolves. Being the world's largest seller of real estate is a totally new experience for Uncle Sam. You can stay ahead of the competition by keeping informed of forthcoming changes in RTC policy.

~ 3 ~

Guidelines for Profitable Investing

What makes a particular property a good investment? A combination of many key factors, or what I like to call *key ingredients*. These ingredients are what you should look for in a profitable real estate investment. They form a solid investment that will pay you dividends for many years to come.

These special ingredients pinpoint exactly what to look for when choosing a good realty investment. People who have succeeded have discovered them and instinctively know how to use them. Without one or more of the five key ingredients, the investment you may be planning could be doomed, or at least its profitability could be seriously impaired.

In short, the five essential ingredients of a good buy are:

1. Buy property that's right for you.
2. Buy at the right price.
3. Buy well-located property in a thriving market.
4. Buy only from motivated sellers.
5. Use the right financing.

BUY PROPERTY THAT'S RIGHT FOR YOU

The top priority in successful realty investing is to buy the right type of property—the one that suits your needs in particular. The best place to get started at distressed-property investment (or, for that matter, nondistressed property in the open market) is to specialize in single-family homes that need fixing up.

Houses that need repair and moderate renovation—what we call handyman's specials—are today's best buy. Why? Because compared to other types of housing, you have a much better chance to make a profit investing in them. Because they need fixing up, you have the opportunity to create value through sweat equity (doing renovations yourself).

Also, there's a plentiful supply and much more demand for single-family homes generally. It's the American dream—what most people want in a home—a place of their own with their own undivided piece of land. They're more versatile and easier to rent or sell. And, in particular, they appreciate in value faster than other types of housing. Sometimes you can even convert them to a more profitable business use.

The Ideal Single-Family Home

What is an ideal single-family home? It's a detached one-family residence built on its own surveyed property with a warranted title and deed (as opposed to a planned development or condominium where owners share a common area). As you know, they're available in a virtually limitless variety of architecture, size, and price range. Eighty percent of the entire residential market consists of single-family homes, while the remainder consists of a variety of other housing, which includes condominiums, cooperatives, apartments, and mobile homes.

With little exception, you should avoid investing in anything that is not a single-family home. Why? Compared to single-family houses, condos and co-ops appreciate slowly, are harder to sell (are frequently overbuilt in many areas), have a limited resale market, have limited or no land at all, and usually are restricted as to usage. (Many condo units have restrictions as to children, owner occupation, and renting.) Mobile homes are not as durable, nor are they likely to appreciate in value.

If you really want to succeed at realty investment, you will have to specialize. And there's no better place to be a specialist than in being a homeowner and learning everything you can about single-family homes. They are, by far, the wisest choice.

Sizable Piece of Land (the More, the Better)

The ideal single-family home is built upon a sizable plot of land. Improvements on the land have value, but these improvements eventually wear out and become obsolete. It's the land itself that endures and appreciates in value. As time passes, it emerges as the most valuable asset, especially for the long-range investor. And it's only fitting that a proper description of such a superior investment be brought forth.

Before there was anything else . . . there was land. It has, and always has had, certain characteristics of unique value. Land has supreme worth because, unlike anything else, it cannot be increased in quantity. Land is required for the production of food and commodities and provides the location to shelter its landlords and tenants. Land provides natural resources, such as lumber, oil, and minerals.

Each plot of land is absolutely different from every other plot of land. Each plot has its own soil quality and underlying composition, its own water supply and drainage ability, its own vegetation and terrain, and its own view. From feudal kings and landlords of the past to the homeowners and developers of today, a measure of one's wealth has been described primarily in the amount of land one owns. Therefore, holding title not necessarily to the improvements that rest upon it, but to the land itself is something precious indeed.

Too little land inhibits the future expansion of a property. Many potential homeowners want more land so they can later add on to the house. Obviously, if there isn't enough land, expansion of the home will be limited; more importantly, the more land you have, the better off you'll be when it comes time to convert the home to another, higher use. For instance, if the home you own can eventually be converted to commercial usage and the land area isn't big enough, the amount of new office space you develop, not to mention the required parking area, will be limited to the small area available.

Without population growth in and around cities, land would have relatively little use beyond its yield of oil, mineral, and agricultural products. Urban land, therefore, becomes valuable primarily because of the services it's able to perform.

These services are measured in the rental amount a tenant is willing to pay for each tract, or what the buyer is willing to give to own a tract that meets his or her needs. Highest rents arise from land used for high-powered retail sales, such as a sprawling urban shopping center. Then come the types of land used for commercial, manufacturing, storage, and residential uses, all of which attract their standards of value through sale and resale and the laws of supply and demand in a community.

If a certain type of land becomes scarce and the demand persists, the price naturally rises until more land of that character becomes available.

The value of land was first brought to my attention twenty years ago when I worked for Wolverine Development in Lansing, Michigan. Back then I was considering the purchase of an eight-unit apartment building, which at the time seemed like a genuine money-maker. The seller was offering attractive terms (no money down), but the building was rather old and the neighborhood wasn't exactly first class. Anyway, I asked my boss, Bruce Maguire, Jr., the owner of the company, for his opinion of the property. These were his comments as we sat in the car looking at the potential investment:

"My first impression is that the building lacks sufficient land. [Except for the land the building was built on and a narrow sidewalk around it, there was no land for tenant parking or potential expansion.] I'll grant you that the present rental income looks attractive, especially since you won't be putting up a down payment, but this is the *only* advantage of owning this property, because it lacks adequate land. Furthermore, the building is at least twenty years old and obviously in some need of repair, which means you'll have to spend a lot of money to maintain the income as well as the property itself."

He also said that I should look at real estate as a long-term investment: "Try to imagine what the property you're investing in will look like and what the neighborhood will be like ten or twenty years from now. This particular property not only lacks sufficient land to expand on, it has an undesirable location. Twenty years from now this neighborhood will likely be a crime-infested slum. Is that what you want to own?"

I learned a lot that day.

To make a long story short, try to get as much land as you can. Over the long term, the primary value of the entire property will be in the land itself.

BUY AT THE RIGHT PRICE

Your overall objective is to determine whether the property is a worthwhile investment. In other words, are you buying value? You must buy the property below market value, then renovate it at moderate cost, and rent it, sell it, live in it, or eventually convert it to a more profitable use.

How do you learn to recognize when a property is under-valued and to estimate costs of needed renovations? You must study the market and become familiar with houses of similar character in the neighborhood where you plan to invest. (Chapter 7 will describe how to evaluate a specific property, including doing inspections for needed renovations.)

Figuring the Maximum-Offer Price

If you can buy foreclosed single-family houses that are in reasonably good condition at 15 percent below the current going rate for similar property, that's usually a bargain. But if the property is run-down and requires a considerable expendi-ture of money and/or time to be made salable, you need a different way to figure what's a bargain. You first have to estimate the costs to renovate the property, then calculate your bargain so that your maximum-offer purchase price plus your estimated renovation costs is 25 percent below the market value of similar real estate.

The maximum-offer purchase price is a predetermined limit or top-dollar figure you're willing to pay for the property. You resolve never to go above this figure, no matter what. Of course, your objective is to purchase a property at a price below this figure.

Why does the maximum-offer purchase price have to be so far below market value? It's because renovations on a fixer-upper will likely cost more and take longer than you estimate. And you may have several reasons for investing in real estate, but your primary objective should be to earn a profit at this venture. To this end, you want your purchase price to give you some assurance that turning a profit is fairly certain.

Here's how you determine the max-offer price. Let's say you know about two similar properties, both single-family houses located in the same neighborhood tract, each having the same square footage with three bedrooms, two baths, and a two-car garage. One house is in move-in condition and sold last month for $160,000. The other house, the property you're considering for purchase, needs new carpeting and floor covering everywhere, a thorough upgrade of the neglected landscaping, and a complete paint job inside and out. Doing some of the renovations yourself, you estimate the fix-up costs at $8,000. Figure 3.1 on page 30 provides a more detailed format for figuring the total cost to acquire and fix up a property.

You'll want the purchase price plus the fix-up costs to be 25 percent less than market value. Since a comparable property in good condition sold last month for $160,000, you can use its selling price as probable market value. If you deduct 25 percent from that figure, the result is a market value of $120,000. From that figure, subtract your $8,000 estimate for fix-up costs, and the result is a max-offer price of $112,000. (Of course, this figure represents the upper limit of what you're willing to pay for a property. The further below this limit you pay, the better the deal you will have made.)

Remember, to be a successful real estate investor, you need to learn how to judge value accurately in order to buy at the right price, to fix up the property, to build equity and earn income with it, and eventually to sell that improved property for a profit.

BUY WELL-LOCATED PROPERTY IN A THRIVING MARKET

What are the ingredients of a good location? That's difficult to say exactly. Some might say it's a place where homeowners can enjoy peace and quiet, have easy access to schools and shopping, and be near good transportation. Others might want to be in the vicinity of public parks or to have a view of the ocean or the mountains.

**FIGURE 3.1   ESTIMATE OF ACQUISITION
AND FIX-UP COSTS**

Address _____
Cost of acquiring property:
   Down payment _____
   Purchasing the deed _____
   Delinquent taxes _____
   Bonds and assessments _____
   Delinquencies on first loan:
      _____ months @ $_____
   Total late charges and fees _____
   Advances _____
   Payoff of second loan (include all
      delinquencies, advances, and fees) _____
Preliminary cost estimates:
   Title and escrow expenses _____
   Loan transfer or origination fee _____
   1 month's P&I and taxes and insurance ____
Total cash to purchase before repairs:
   Balance of all loans after purchase _____
   Other encumbrances _____
Total property cost before repairs:
   Estimated cost of repairs:
      Paint _____ Plumbing _____ Roof _____
      Electrical ____ Termite ____ Fencing ____
      Landscape ___ Floors ___ Carpeting ___
      Wallpaper ___ Fixtures ___ Hardware ___
Total estimated cost of repairs: _____
Total property cost after repairs: _____

Locations to Avoid

Instead of what to *look for* in a location, sometimes it's better to be aware of what to *avoid* in a location. Before investing in a residential property, ask the following questions, which will alert you to what to avoid in the selection of a particular property:

- Is the house next to commercial buildings? Industrial and commercial buildings should be located within proper or conforming zoning. Likewise, residential property should be properly located in the midst of other residential property. This is what's known as conformity.
- Is the house near an airport or under the flight path of noisy aircraft?
- Is the house next to a school playground, where excessive noise may interfere with the quiet enjoyment of the premises?
- Is the house adjacent to a cemetery or undertaker?
- Does an unusual volume of vehicular traffic pass by that may prove to be a nuisance?
- Is the property lowland and subject to flooding?

While most of these characteristics enhance a commercial location, they all seriously detract from the value of a residential property.

Thriving Market

Now for the second part of this key ingredient: Is the property in a thriving market? A thriving market is anything that's not declining in terms of population, employment, and overall property values.

For instance, a nonthriving market, or declining area, could be the city of Houston, Texas, during the 1980s. During this time, Houston experienced what economists call a "rolling recession." When a glut of petroleum supplies on the world market caused oil prices to fall drastically, oil companies cut back on employment, and many related businesses failed. Also, many banks failed during this time, partially because many unemployed people living in Houston could no longer make payments on their real estate loans. The result was an over-supply of new housing and foreclosures, which most people couldn't afford to buy. Eventually, the value of housing in Houston plummeted because of this rolling recession. Obviously, you'd want to avoid investing in stricken areas that are experiencing such an economic downturn.

Also be careful when investing in smaller urban areas that depend primarily on one type of industry. If employers in that industry experience bad economic times or have to close, the surrounding area will probably become depressed. On the other hand, areas that have diverse industries, such as Los Angeles or Boston, are likely to thrive even if a major industry fails.

BUY ONLY FROM MOTIVATED SELLERS

A motivated seller (sometimes referred to as a "don't-wanter") is someone who, because of certain circumstances, is prepared to sell at below market value. Such circumstances might include divorce, death in the family, job relocation, loss of employment, vacant rentals and associated landlord headaches, lack of money, or another property bought and ready to move to. If you have any combination of these factors, the seller will be extremely motivated and prepared to look at just about any offer.

Remember that you're a pennies-on-the-dollar investor, not

someone who is willing to pay full market value for property. A seller who is not motivated to sell is unlikely to accept anything less than what the property is worth. (More information about negotiating with a seller is available in Chapter 8.)

USE THE RIGHT FINANCING

Good financing is critical to real estate profits because acquiring the wrong type inevitably will prove costly, and could even inhibit the resale of your property. Essentially, deciding what type of financing is best for you boils down to choosing between a fixed-rate and a variable-rate mortgage. But there are plenty of other options, and that's because innovative lenders in today's ever-changing marketplace are offering a wide variety of financing.

Borrowing money to buy real estate is, no doubt, critical to making profitable investments. But did you know that the amount you borrow—meaning the amount of leverage you apply to the investment—has a definite effect on your investment yield? And did you know that sometimes you don't have to originate new financing? Instead, you can assume certain types of existing loans and save $30,000 or more doing it. The next chapter will discuss all these topics, plus a lot more.

OTHER GENERAL GUIDELINES

Beyond the five key ingredients are additional investor guidelines that should prove helpful:

- Before going ahead with such a substantial undertaking as purchasing real estate, ask yourself these questions: Is the property a good deal? Could I sell it tomorrow and at least break even?
- Study real estate. Be a keen student of residential

property, with special emphasis on single-family houses.
Become familiar with market activity in your
neighborhood, and read everything available on
investing in real estate.

- Have enough funds or rainy-day money to make
substantial payments. This protects against
unforeseeable difficulty, such as vacancies, unusual
expenses, or periods of unemployment. The
recommended amount is the equivalent of three months'
salary in savings to draw from in such an emergency.

- Have staying power or willingness to be patient so that
your investment can ripen with age. Remember, to get
the most from realty investing, you must be prepared
for the long term.

- If not thoroughly skilled at a certain investment
technique, be wise enough to associate yourself with a
learned Realtor. Likewise, before attempting unfamiliar
renovations, hire or become the partner of a competent
tradesperson.

- Learn to walk before you run. In other words, you
become educated through the process of reading and
gaining experience. And you pay your dues by
consummating small deals before plunging into big ones
that take more money, involve greater risks, and require
more skill and experience.

Things do go awry. Let's face it, Murphy was right when he
said, "If anything can go wrong, it will." But if you're forewarned of what can go wrong, you can often make contingency plans and overcome the setbacks.

Some ways things can go awry are from underestimating
renovation costs, overappraising completed value, overappraising investment before renovation, being unable to sell or rent
the renovated investment, and having loans promised but

never funded, which often results in loss of the earnest-money deposit. You can avoid most of these pitfalls if you prepare properly.

Some problems, unfortunately, cannot be avoided—for example, the unsalability of your renovated property. But this is one of the risks of being an entrepreneur. You have to assume a certain amount of risk. Remember, anyone can earn 5 percent interest in a risk-free savings account.

The trick to succeeding is to eliminate or reduce most of the risk associated with your potential investment. This includes accurately appraising the property's value before renovation. It also entails accurately evaluating the cost of such renovation. Then, after purchasing the property, make good use of it while either living in it, renting it, or selling it.

Have a contingency—an out, so to say—for alternative usage of the property, just in case everything doesn't go as planned. If the property goes unsold, you could, for example, move into the property yourself (and rent your present residence) or, for the time being, rent out the unsold property until market conditions improve. The idea is to plan for the best but prepare for the worst.

Finally, bear in mind that when it comes to profitable investing in real estate, the essential ingredients never change.

~ 4 ~

Financing: What's Available and How to Get It

Not too long ago, financing a home was cut and dried. Lenders offered a basic fixed-rate, thirty-year loan. Nowadays the borrower has a variety of creative mortgage loans to choose from.

INTRODUCTION TO THE POSSIBILITIES

Potential homeowners today can practically design their own mortgage from a virtual maze of choices—fifteen-, twenty-, or thirty-year payoffs and various types of adjustable loans, such as two-step and convertible.

Home buyers also have certain advantages that did not exist before. They can buy with very little or sometimes with no money down. In certain cases they can even avoid originating a new loan entirely by assuming a property owner's existing loan. (Read more about assuming mortgages later in this chapter.)

Home buyers also have to decide on what type of interest payment they want. They have a choice of adjustable or fixed rate. Some lenders offer a convertible loan (an adjustable-rate mortgage that can convert to a fixed rate).

But what type of loan is best for you? How much should you

borrow and for how long? An ill-advised decision could be costly, in the neighborhood of perhaps $30,000 or more in lost savings on the purchase of just one property!

This chapter will try to save you money as well as explain some of the complexities and options in the ever-changing world of real estate finance. In case you're unfamiliar with the jargon used in the industry today, the following explanations about financing a home should prove helpful.

Mortgage

When you borrow money to buy real estate, you (the *mortgagor*) retain title to the acquired property, but you give a mortgage to the lender (the *mortgagee*). The *mortgage* secures the loan; it says the lender can take title to the property if you fail to make payments on the mortgage loan.

To get title, the lender must *foreclose* on the loan. During the foreclosure process, which can take six months or longer, you, the mortgagor, still own the property. You can rescue the property before the foreclosure sale by making all payments that are due (including penalties), refinancing with another lender, or selling. Title to the property reverts to the new buyer when the property has been sold at a foreclosure sale, or to the lender if no one buys it, and you no longer own it.

Trust Deed

A trust deed serves the purpose of a mortgage contract, but title to your property is held by a neutral third party (neither you nor the lender), called the *trustee*, usually a title insurance company. If the borrower (the *trustor*) fails to make loan payments, the lender (*beneficiary*) can order the trustee to begin the foreclosure process and eventually get title through a trustee sale (a foreclosure sale). Compared to the more

cumbersome mortgage loans, trust deed loans are more efficiently foreclosed on—sometimes in as little as ninety days.

Second Mortgage or Second Trust Deed

If you already have a mortgage on your property but borrow
again, your new loan is secured by a *second mortgage* or trust
deed. This loan would be second in line for payoff at a foreclosure sale. A first mortgagee has greater priority for receiving
the proceeds of the sale. The holder of the second mortgage or
second trust deed can collect proceeds only after the money
owed on the first recorded loan is paid out.

A second loan is said to be *junior* to a first loan, meaning it
is listed (recorded in the county records) behind or after a first
loan. Since a second loan is riskier than a first loan (less
security for the lender), interest rates for secondary financing
are considerably higher.

Interest

Interest is the rate charged by the lender for the use of money.
Interest on real estate loans is usually expressed as a percent-
age charged against the money owed (principal balance). If
you borrowed $100,000 to buy a house at 10.5 percent, you
would pay about $10,500 interest in the first year. In the
second year, however, interest charges would be reduced,
since interest is computed on the principal remaining after the
previous year's payments. Such a gradual payoff of the principal over a stated period of time (the *term*) is called *amortiza-
tion*.

Surprisingly, the cost of a house is much less than the
interest paid to finance the purchase of that house. For example, suppose you buy a $100,000 house and borrow $80,000 at
10.5 percent for thirty years. That mortgage, if paid off over

the entire thirty years, will cost you about $183,000 in interest—more than double the amount you borrowed, and almost double the price of your house! That's not even counting the $80,000 in principal that you have to pay back. In other words, in a period of thirty years, you actually pay $283,000 for a $100,000 house.

What's considered a reasonable rate of interest to pay? In today's market, 10 percent is thought of as the median rate to pay on a first mortgage loan. Any rate below 10 percent is considered good, while a rate above it is considered costly or excessive.

Fixed Rate vs. Adjustable Rate

Most lenders offer the borrower a choice in the way interest is computed—a fixed or an adjustable rate (called ARM for adjustable-rate mortgage). The interest rate on the ARM is periodically adjusted up or down, while interest on the fixed-rate loan remains at a constant rate over the loan's term.

ARMs can be originated at initial lower, teaser rates but then are periodically adjusted (mostly upward). Typically, you could originate an ARM at 7.5 percent for the first year, then the rate is allowed to go up but not to exceed a certain limit, such as 13.5 percent.

Which is better, the fixed or adjustable rate? The answer depends on how long you intend to own the property. Considering that market interest rates historically are, more often than not, in a rising trend, the adjustable rate is better for loans held for a short term—five years or less. For longer than five years, the fixed-rate mortgage is better. Here's why:

- Fixed-rate mortgages are less risky. That's because you have peace of mind, knowing the monthly payment remains constant over the mortgage term.

- Over a duration of five years or more, the interest cost of the adjustable-rate mortgage generally exceeds that of the fixed-rate mortgage.

Adjustable rates are better than fixed rates only under the following situations:

- When the term of the mortgage is five years or less. That's because it takes about five years for the initial lower adjustable rate to overtake the higher fixed rate.
- When market interest rates are primarily in a declining trend.
- When the adjustable rate has the option to convert to a fixed rate.

Convertible Mortgage

A convertible mortgage is a home loan with an adjustable rate that can convert to a fixed-rate loan. It gives you the best of both worlds—the lower initial rates of the ARM and the option to lock in a fixed rate at some future time. Most lenders charge a conversion fee for this advantageous option.

Two-Step Mortgage

One of the latest innovations should appeal to home buyers who expect to move in seven years but want the security of a fixed-rate mortgage in case they don't. Similar to the convertible loan, the two-step mortgage starts out with an adjustable rate, but after seven years a fixed rate automatically kicks in. After the one-time change, the loan remains at a fixed rate for the remaining twenty-three years of a thirty-year term. Unlike paying certain fees associated with refinancing or converting a mortgage, the borrower would pay no additional fees at readjustment time.

Loan Assumption

Instead of financing the purchase of your home with a costly new mortgage, often, especially in moderately priced neighborhoods, you can assume the seller's loan and save $30,000 or more doing it. Assumption of a loan means the buyer pays off the seller's equity and takes over payments and responsibility to the lender. Here's why loan assumption can be a great idea:

- You avoid the costly bank charges required to originate a new loan. These charges are in the form of points and incidental fees, which when added up can cost about 4 percent of the amount being borrowed. Under a loan assumption, you pay only a small assumption fee of around $50.
- You save on interest charges over the term of the loan because, in most cases, the loan being assumed has a much lower interest rate than is being offered on new loans.
- No credit qualification is required on most assumable mortgages. There's a shorter closing time—only a few days, not the sixty or ninety days it takes to originate most mortgage loans.
- The loan will again be assumable when you decide to sell, making your property more appealing to prospective buyers.

What are the best assumable mortgages? Some of the older, more mature VA and FHA mortgages are the best. *Note:* At one time, almost all VA and FHA loans were fully assumable. *This is not the case anymore.* Abuse by certain unworthy individuals has led to restrictions on the assumability of most VA and FHA loans being originated nowadays. Be sure someone verifies whether or not a loan is assumable.

Points

Depending on the situation, *points* (also referred to as *discount points*) are a service fee lenders often charge to increase their yield on the principal borrowed. One point equals 1 percent of the principal. A fee of two points on a $100,000 loan will cost you $2,000. Sometimes the lender will add the cost of points to the principal. Thus, in the example, you'd pay interest on $102,000, although you received a loan of only $100,000. At other times the lender deducts, or discounts, the points from the loan proceeds. As an example, on a $100,000 loan with two points, you would receive only $98,000 when the loan is funded.

Loan Origination Fee

Lenders charge a *loan origination fee* to cover certain administrative costs. This fee also makes their loans more lucrative (increases yield). Usually included in this fee are such items as points and the cost of an appraisal and credit report. Do not confuse the loan origination fee with a *loan application fee*, which is a minimal charge some lenders levy the borrower when he or she applies for a loan.

Loan-to-Value Ratio

The loan-to-value ratio compares the amount of the loan to the property's value. This ratio determines the amount of money the lender is willing to lend. Lenders usually determine a maximum loan-to-value ratio based on appraised value, not the property's asking price or selling price. If the lender will loan 80 percent of value, the buyer must come up with the down payment of 20 percent.

Federal Housing Administration (FHA)

The Federal Housing Administration (FHA) is a branch of the Department of Housing and Urban Development. It assists potential home buyers by offering low-cost financing to the general public, sometimes with as little as 5 percent down. The FHA does not actually lend the buyer money; instead, it encourages lending by insuring the lender against default. The buyer pays a small monthly premium for the insurance.

Veterans Administration (VA)

The Veterans Administration (VA), part of the Department of Veterans Affairs, helps qualified veterans acquire home financing. It offers 100 percent financing at below-market interest rates. Like the FHA, the VA does not actually fund the loan. It guarantees the loan to the lender that holds the mortgage.

Private Mortgage Insurance (PMI)

Lenders can also protect themselves by having borrowers purchase private mortgage insurance (PMI), which is available from private insurers. The purpose of PMI is to enable home buyers to purchase with minimal down payments. As loans for more than 80 percent of the purchase price are considered more risky, lenders often require borrowers to buy PMI if their down payment is less than 20 percent.

Due-on-Sale Clause

Many mortgage contracts contain a due-on-sale clause, which says the total amount remaining on a loan is due when the property is sold. In essence, this clause prevents the buyer from assuming the loan. In the absence of a due-on-sale clause, a loan is assumable, as described earlier.

Lis Pendens (Notice of Action)

A *lis pendens* is the legal term for a legal notice that a lawsuit is pending on the subject property. It gives notice that anyone acquiring an interest in the property after the date of notice may be bound by the outcome of the pending litigation. A foreclosure sale usually does not cancel out this pending litigation, unlike most other liens and attachments on real property.

Rescission

The act of nullifying the foreclosure process is called *rescission*. It places the property back to its previous condition, before the default was recorded. Recording a rescission removes the default from the title records.

GETTING A MORTGAGE LOAN

When buying distressed property at auction, you have two choices: either take the financing with you, or get financing from the seller, which also includes getting it from someone (a mortgage broker, for example) who arranges financing in behalf of the seller.

How Much Should You Borrow?

Generally, the bigger your mortgage (the more leverage you have), the better your realty investment. There are four big pluses for the use of a mortgage:

1. Compared to paying all cash, the rate of return is much greater using leverage. If you pay cash for a $50,000 house, and you sell the house in one year for $55,000, you will earn $5,000, or a 10 percent return on your $50,000 investment. But if you leverage the investment with a $5,000 down payment and sell one year later for a $5,000 profit, you will earn a 100% return on your $5,000 investment.
2. It preserves valuable cash reserves, which you can use later to renovate the purchased property.
3. It allows you to liquefy, or refinance, home equity for higher-return investments—a second house, for example.
4. Tax-deductible equity loans can be used to pay off nondeductible consumer loans.

Leverage

One way to think of leverage is that it's using other people's money to gain a greater return on your investment. You unleash the powers of wealth creation when leverage is applied to any realty investment. The use of credit (proper or otherwise), particularly using leverage to enhance your investment yield, is an American way of life.

If you have any negative thoughts about borrowing money to buy real estate, forget them. In the business world, particularly within the realm of real property ownership, success is often measured not by what you have, but by what you owe! This, of course, does not mean that you should overextend yourself to the point where your total debts are greater than your net worth.

Anyone can earn a risk-free 5 percent in a savings account. But it takes someone special—someone skilled, someone willing to supplement his or her education—to consistently earn

50 percent or more investing in real estate. The only way to accomplish this high rate of return is to apply maximum leverage to your realty investments.

How Much House Can You Afford?

How much house you can afford depends on a lot of things. Married couples with children can afford one amount, single people usually can afford to pay proportionately more of their income toward the purchase of a home.

As a rule, couples with children should not exceed 28 percent of their gross monthly income for the house payment, including the cost of principal and interest, property taxes, and hazard insurance. Single people and married couples without children usually can afford up to 33 percent of gross monthly income for a house payment.

Institutional lenders require a range of 25 to 33 percent of the borrower's gross monthly income as the limit for the house payment. They allow the upper limits only when the borrowers have no other consumer debt outstanding, such as money owing on credit cards or a car loan. Institutional lenders know from experience what it takes to avoid potential financial difficulties. Therefore, it is wise to maintain your house payments within these limits, no matter how you acquire the loan.

Estimating Monthly Payments

Tables 4.1 and 4.2 on pages 48 and 49 illustrate required monthly payments at selected interest rates for thirty- and fifteen-year fixed-rate loans. To use the tables, first select the loan amount in the left column, then go across the top and select the appropriate interest rate. Where the loan amount and interest rate intersect is the monthly payment for principal and interest (P&I) that you will pay to amortize, or pay off, the loan.

Table 4.3 on page 50 illustrates the monthly mortgage cost of borrowing $1,000 for fifteen-year and thirty-year fully amortized loans at different interest rates. As an example, if you wanted to know the monthly mortgage cost of a $12,000 loan at 11 percent for thirty years, first look at the column for 11 percent. Then select the thirty-year row. The factor is $9.53. To find your monthly payment on $12,000, multiply $9.53 by 12, which results in a monthly payment of $114.36.

Qualifying for a Mortgage Loan

Conventional loans usually can be processed in 30 days if there are no unforeseen delays. However, VA and FHA loans can take anywhere from 60 to 120 days, owing to bureaucratic red tape and additional inspections and procedures required on these loans. Whatever the case, you can help speed up the loan approval process by carefully obtaining and submitting information required by the lender. A later section of this chapter suggests ways to speed loan approval.

When you initiate the loan request, the lender will start the process by having you fill out a loan application. If you have all the pertinent information required on the loan application, go ahead and fill it out completely. If not, take the application home, fill it out, and either mail it or personally return it to the lender.

In addition to the loan application, you will be required to sign an employment verification form. The lender will then submit this signed form to your employer to verify employment. If you are self-employed, you will have to supply the lender with federal income tax returns for the past two years and a profit and loss statement since your last tax filing.

**TABLE 4.1   30-YEAR FIXED MONTHLY PAYMENT
(P&I) AT SELECTED INTEREST RATES**

Amount ($)	Interest Rate (%)										
	8.0	8.5	9.0	9.5	10.0	11.0	12.0	13.0	14.0
60,000	$440	$461	$483	$505	$527	$571	$ 617	$ 664	$ 711
70,000	514	538	563	589	614	667	720	774	829
80,000	587	615	644	673	702	762	823	885	948
90,000	660	693	724	757	790	857	926	996	1,086
100,000	734	771	805	841	878	952	1,029	1,106	1,189

**TABLE 4.2   15-YEAR FIXED MONTHLY PAYMENT
(P&I) AT SELECTED INTEREST RATES**

Amount ($)	Interest Rate (%)										
	8.0	8.5	9.0	9.5	10.0	11.0	12.0	13.0	14.0
60,000	$573	$591	$ 609	$ 627	$ 645	$ 682	$ 720	$ 759	$ 799
70,000	669	689	710	731	752	796	840	886	932
80,000	765	788	811	835	860	909	960	1,012	1,065
90,000	860	886	913	940	967	1,023	1,080	1,139	1,199
100,000	956	985	1,014	1,044	1,075	1,137	1,200	1,265	1,322

**TABLE 4.3   MONTHLY FIXED PAYMENT (P&I) COST
PER $1,000 AT SELECTED INTEREST RATES**

Term	Interest Rate (%)								
	8.0	8.5	9.0	9.5	10.0	11.0	12.0	13.0	14.0
15 years	$9.56	$9.85	$10.15	$10.45	$10.75	$11.37	$12.01	$12.66	$13.32
30 years	7.34	7.69	8.05	8.41	8.78	9.53	10.29	11.07	11.85

From the information on the loan application, the lender will order a credit report. Once the lender has the credit report, he or she will carefully scrutinize the data supplied. If your credit is not approved, you will be informed immediately of the bad news.

Upon receiving the appraisal and credit report, the lender will analyze both, then determine the maximum amount you can borrow on the property. Next, the lender takes into account your income to determine whether the calculated monthly payment falls within stipulated guidelines. (Remember, a maximum of 28 percent of your gross monthly income is allowed for principal, interest, taxes, and insurance, or a maximum of 33 percent if you have no other liabilities.) If the payment is within the guidelines, you will be informed of this amount and the amount of points and interest rate the lender will charge.

In certain cases, the loan process entails additional steps. The VA and FHA require a property inspection in order to determine whether the property meets certain minimum standards. Also, some states require a termite inspection of the property.

Term of the Loan

Which is better, a fifteen-year or a thirty-year mortgage? The fifteen-year fixed-rate loan is ideal for those who can afford the higher monthly payments (see Table 4.4). These higher monthly payments will save tens of thousands of dollars in interest compared to a thirty-year payoff (see Table 4.5). Furthermore, you'll enjoy faster equity buildup and the satisfaction of owning your home unencumbered (free and clear of any mortgages) in half the time it takes with a thirty-year mortgage.

**TABLE 4.4   COMPARISON OF 15- AND 30-YEAR
LOANS AT SELECTED RATES OF INTEREST**
(Loan Amount of $70,000)

Interest Rate (%)	Payment Required	
	15-Year Loan	30-Year Loan
8.0	$669	$514
8.5	689	538
9.0	710	563
9.5	731	589
10.0	752	614
10.5	774	640
11.0	796	667
12.0	840	720
13.0	886	774
14.0	932	829

**TABLE 4.5   ACCUMULATED EQUITY AND INTEREST
PAID ON 15- AND 30-YEAR LOANS**
(Contract Interest Rate of 10 Percent,
Loan Amount of $70,000)

Time	15-Year Accumulated		30-Year Accumulated	
	Interest Paid	Equity Earned	Interest Paid	Equity Earned
After 5 years	$32,044	$13,090	$ 34,479	$ 2,380
After 15 years	65,401	70,000	97,766	12,810
After 30 years	—	—	151,152	70,000

Besides the burden of higher monthly payments, the only other disadvantage of the shorter-term mortgage is that interest deductions for tax purposes are much less than with a thirty-year mortgage.

Where to Start

Once you have an idea of what type of mortgage you want, it's time to start thinking about where to get it. If you're already a customer of a savings and loan institution, start there. However, do not accept the first loan offered. Make a few calls to other S&Ls and compare all the costs.

Savings and loan institutions are the primary source of long-term residential loans. Other sources of residential mortgage money include mortgage bankers, loan brokers (who may represent certain S&Ls), and credit unions. Lending by commercial banks traditionally is more short-term in nature, funding auto loans, credit card accounts, and personal loans.

Besides calling other S&Ls in your area, check the local newspaper for quotations. Quite often all the local lenders, along with their quoted rates and fees, can be found in the business section. In addition, make a few calls to mortgage bankers and real estate brokers, who may have insight into who is offering the best deals. Remember, just a reduction of half a percent in interest can save you thousands of dollars over the life of a long-term mortgage.

When you're inquiring about mortgage loans, compare more than just interest rates. Ask about the other charges you will have to pay. These include points, origination fee, application fee, cost of appraisal and credit report, and, if applicable, the conversion fee.

Also, beware of rate fluctuations. How long will the rate you're applying for be locked in? Most lenders will charge one point to lock in their quoted rate for a stated period of time.

Questions Asked of You

The mortgage lender you select is primarily interested in three things. Do you have the down payment? Are you creditworthy? And can you afford the monthly payments, which include principal, interest, taxes, and hazard insurance?

Besides making these primary inquiries, your lender will also require you to answer other pertinent questions. On the loan application are questions about income, debts, bank balance, marital status, and number of dependents. The following questions are commonly asked on the loan application:

- Are there any outstanding judgments against you?
- Have you ever been foreclosed on, or given a deed in lieu of foreclosure?
- Have you ever been bankrupt?
- Are you borrowing any part of the down payment?
- Are you obligated to pay alimony or child support?
- Are you a comaker or endorser of a note?

Speeding Loan Approval

Although taking out a mortgage loan can be a tedious, time-consuming task, you can speed up the process by being prepared. Start with your credit history. If you're unsure of it, check it out with a national credit reporting agency. This way there will be no surprises. Any negative data that appear on the credit report will require an explanation.

As mentioned earlier, self-employed applicants will need copies of federal income tax returns for the past two years, so have these ready. If you work for someone else, you'll sign an employment verification form to be sent to your employer. To speed up that process, inform the person at your company who is responsible for verification that the inquiry is coming, and have it sent to that particular person.

Having information ahead of time also speeds up the approval process. You'll need all the appropriate account numbers for bank accounts, credit cards, outstanding loans, and previously paid loans. You'll also need to submit the addresses and branch names for these accounts.

Questions You Should Ask

A home—for your own residence or an investment—is a costly purchase, and you will be contracting for terms over a substantial period of time. Thus, it is very important that you become fully informed of exactly what you're committing yourself to. When comparing mortgage loans and lenders, use the following important questions as a guide:

- Is there a prepayment penalty? (Lenders often charge a penalty of six months' interest for premature payoff of a mortgage.) If so, how much do I have to pay for prematurely paying off the mortgage?
- Is there an impound account to cover the cost of taxes and insurance?
- Is the loan assumable? If so, does the lender have the right to raise the interest rate upon assumption?
- If PMI is charged, when can I stop paying for it?
- If the loan is adjustable, when and what are the rate adjustments?
- If the loan is convertible, how much is the conversion fee, and when can I convert to a fixed rate?

~ 5 ~

Foreclosed Property: Where to Find It and How to Buy It

Today's investor in distressed property has a virtual smorgasbord of foreclosed property to choose from. The largest selection is from among the foreclosed assets of the busted thrifts, some of which are being auctioned off by the RTC. Investors also have the opportunity to buy the foreclosed assets of thriving S&Ls or to buy from several federal agencies, including HUD. Furthermore, investors can invest in any one of three phases through which foreclosure property may pass.

THE THREE PHASES OF FORECLOSURE

As stated in the previous chapter, mortgages and trust deeds are financial instruments that create liens against real property. These instruments state that, should the borrower default on the loan, the lender has the legal right to sell the encumbered property in order to satisfy the loan obligation in a foreclosure sale. In about half the states, a mortgage is used as security against default, while in the others, borrowers use a trust deed. Although the phases of foreclosure are similar for both security instruments, the following descriptions about these phases pertain to *trust deed proceedings only*. Before buying property in foreclosure, learn the specific procedures used in your state.

The Default Phase

The first phase is the default period. The lender initiates foreclosure proceedings by sending the borrower a notice of default, after having sent numerous requests for payment and written warnings of eventual foreclosure should the borrower not correct the delinquent condition immediately. At the request of the lender, the trustee records the notice of default, in effect giving notice to the public that the loan is in default. The actual recording of the notice takes place at the county recorder's office in the county in which the property is located. The notice includes essential data pertaining to the trust deed, the amount in arrears, the address of the property, and the date of recording.

In California the owner/trustor has ninety days from the date of recording of the notice of default to reinstate the loan (to make the loan current by paying all payments in arrears, including late charges or other penalties). The law requires the lender to accept the trustor's reinstatement money during this ninety-day period.

If the trustor has not reinstated the loan within the specified period, the lender has the right to notify the trustee to publish a notice of trustee's sale. This published notice states that the subject property will be sold at public auction to the highest bidder at a given date and place in that county. In California the actual date of sale is at least twenty-one days after the ninety-day reinstatement period.

During this twenty-one-day period, referred to as the publication period, the lender has the right to refuse reinstatement of the loan and can demand payment in full of the principal amount owing. Often, lenders will allow reinstatement during the publication period, depending on the history of the loan or how the current market interest rate compares with the rate attached to the loan in arrears. If the rate of interest being charged on the loan is significantly lower than current market rates, the lender may be encouraged to proceed with the foreclosure sale and relend the proceeds at a higher rate of interest.

The Foreclosure Sale Phase

If the property owner fails to pay the lender all moneys in arrears during the reinstatement period, the property enters phase two, the actual foreclosure sale. The sale is a public auction held by the lender, or an agent (the trustee) of the lender, at which time the property will be sold to the highest bidder. Usually the trustee initiates the bidding, beginning with the minimum acceptable bid, which is often set at the principal amount owing plus all incidental late fees and penalties. Proceeds from the sale are disbursed to all lien holders in order of the priority of their recorded loans. This particular phase of the foreclosure process requires that the successful bidder pay full bid price for the property in cash.

The Real Estate Owned (REO) Phase

If no one buys the foreclosed property at the foreclosure sale, it enters the third phase and becomes a possession of the lender. Should that lender be a financial institution, the property is placed in inventory as REO. It is valued at the amount of loan principal owing plus all other costs and fees pertinent to the foreclosure sale. Once the lender takes possession, the property is usually secured (boarded up to keep mischievous intruders out), evaluated, and listed for sale.

Acquisition Tactics in Each Phase

Buying from the Owner During the Default Phase

Assuming there's enough equity in the property and thereby potential for profit, the objective of buying from an owner in default is to gain title to the property and reinstate the loan in default (paying all money in arrears) before the foreclosure sale occurs. This, of course, must happen during the reinstatement period; otherwise the lender can reject the payment and proceed with the foreclosure sale.

This method is not as neat and clean as buying at the foreclosure sale because you have to be concerned with all the other recorded liens held against the property. In other words, if you acquire the property before the foreclosure sale, the property is still security for outstanding recorded liens held against it. Only the actual foreclosure sale cancels out these liens.

Let's say that you've been thumbing through the notices of default published in the paper, and you find an interesting prospect. The amount in arrears is $60,000, and you know that homes in that particular neighborhood sell for $100,000. Under the assumption there are no other liens held against the property, you can conclude that there is $40,000 equity.

Your objective in this example would be to try to buy that equity at a discount, so to speak, and thereby earn a profit. You can do that by assuming the existing loan or, if it's not assumable, getting a new loan and paying it off, then having the owner convey title to you. What you pay for the $40,000 equity is very negotiable.

But what if there is a second loan (or third, back taxes, etc.) on the property? Then you'll have to find out exactly what is owed against the property. This will require research, such as thumbing through the county records and paying for a title search.

Sooner or later, you will have to meet and negotiate with the owner of the property in distress. Simply make an appointment; avoid discussing details over the phone. A personal visit to the property not only allows you to get details about how much is owed, it also gives you the opportunity to meet the owner and look over the property.

Here, time is of the essence. For you, the investor, time is an ally. But the owners are under pressure to remedy the situation, or else lose the property along with their good credit rating. Remember that you can save the owners disgrace (the black mark of a foreclosure on their credit rating) by allowing you to bail them out and at the same time realize some cash for their equity.

Buying at the Foreclosure Sale

You can obtain information about foreclosure sales from subscription services, legal newspapers, and local newspapers that are authorized to publish such legal notices. Further legalities require the trustee to post the notice of trustee (foreclosure) sale on one or more public buildings within the same county and on the subject property itself. Thus, you'll often see these postings on bulletin boards in your county courthouse.

The best strategy for bidding at an open auction similar to a foreclosure sale is to be totally prepared. Know in advance how much you plan to bid, and do not allow yourself to exceed this predetermined price. You lose nothing if you don't buy at all. On the other hand, it is possible to get caught up in the frenzy of competitive bidding and pay much more for the property than you ever intended.

But before you can successfully bid at the foreclosure sale, you should already have prepared a detailed analysis of the property. Besides having a predetermined maximum price, this includes knowing the minimum acceptable bid; making a thorough inspection, including an estimate of cost for renovations and repairs; and evaluating the fair market value. (The next chapter provides a more detailed description of guidelines for buying at an auction/foreclosure sale.)

Either the trustee or his or her agent will oversee the foreclosure sale. By this time the lender/beneficiary has instructed the trustee as to what will be the minimum opening bid. Most often this figure is the total amount owed the lender, including the principal, late fees, and penalties.

Successful bidders will be required to pay for the property either in cash or by cashier's check. Personal checks are not acceptable. Just before the sale, the trustee usually asks to see the money or cashier's check of those who will be bidding. This is an attempt to qualify those who have a serious interest in the property, as opposed to those who are present merely as spectators. Astonishing as it may seem, public foreclosure sales attract many onlookers who have no intention of bidding.

When the minimum acceptable bid is high, there's limited interest by bidders because of the greater amount of cash required to buy. When the minimum acceptable bid is low, more bidders will be attracted to the sale.

Finally, while attending a foreclosure sale, be wary of a bidder who may attempt to make a deal with you. Unscrupulous bidders have been known to pay off other potential bidders before the sale in an attempt to eliminate the competition so they can purchase the property for the minimum bid price.

Buying REO

As mentioned earlier in the book, REO is usually sold through preferred Realtors and to investors the lender has done business with before. REO departments shy away from random calls by the public. However, if you're interested, approach the REO department in person, meet its manager, and explain exactly what it is you're looking for. Establishing such a personal relationship is the only practical way to have access to these potential bargains.

One aspect of REO makes it a superior investment compared to real estate in the other phases. In most cases, the act of foreclosure clears the title of all liens on the property that existed before the sale, with the exception of certain superior liens (such as property tax liens). Once the lender has possession of the property, the lender owns it free and clear. This means that if you acquire REO, it will be free of any problems except for overdue property taxes (which the lender is obligated to pay) and deferred maintenance.

There are other advantages to investing in a lender's REO. Because they're in the business of lending, not property management, lenders are usually eager to unload the property. Investors can often purchase it far below market value at very good financial terms. Since the seller is also the lender, favorable interest rates are often available without the cost of points. It is also possible to defer the first mortgage payment from one to three months after acquiring title to the property. In many cases, especially when buying REO from institutional lenders, you can often arrange for the lender you're buying the property from to loan you enough to make the renovations. Finally, the lender will frequently handle most of the closing costs, since lenders usually have escrow facilities available in-house. (Your ability to benefit from these advantages will depend on how shrewd a negotiator you are and how good a working relationship you have with the REO manager.)

SOURCES OF DISTRESSED PROPERTY

Besides buying from the borrower or lender during any of the three phases of foreclosure, you also have several other viable sources. These include tax foreclosure sales, the Resolution Trust Corporation, the Department of Housing and Urban Development, and auctions of surplus property.

Tax Foreclosure Sales

In Florida (your state may have a similar procedure), failure to pay real property taxes results in the public sale of a tax certificate. Investors in these certificates not only earn a high rate of interest, they also may eventually be able to assume ownership of the property for the mere cost of the certificate. This method also benefits the county by generating tax revenue immediately.

Here's how it works: Real property taxes become delinquent on April 1. After that, the county publishes (usually in a local newspaper) a list of the delinquent properties and the amount of unpaid taxes on them. The county annually issues tax certificates for the amount of the unpaid taxes and holds a tax certificate auction. The certificates are auctioned to investors for the value of the unpaid taxes plus a small processing fee. When property owners pay the taxes, they also must pay the certificate holder interest at a rate that is set at the auction at a maximum of 18 percent, with bids driving it lower. (The tax certificate goes to the *low* bidder.)

If property owners fail to pay the delinquent taxes within two years, certificate holders may apply (petition) for a tax deed. This triggers a tax foreclosure sale, with the property going to the highest bidder. The tax certificate is paid off with interest from the proceeds of the sale. If no one bids for the property, the certificate holder assumes the property. The certificates expire after seven years, which means the certificate holders will lose their investment if they don't petition the county to auction the property.

The best strategy here is first to study the published list, then to invest only in the certificates of property you'd be interested in owning. You should, for example, avoid buying certificates for land that is practically worthless, such as platted lots in thirty-year-old subdivisions that were never developed.

The Resolution Trust Corporation (RTC)

Another great source of investment is the distressed property of insolvent S&Ls now under the jurisdiction of the Resolution Trust Corporation (RTC). The RTC currently has over $300 billion in property up for sale, and that amount will surely expand as more institutions continue to falter.

Every six months the RTC prints its inventory publication, containing over forty thousand properties nationwide. The list of residential properties located within certain regions can be purchased for $15 by calling the RTC direct at (800) 431-0600.

In addition to this semiannual publication, the RTC also offers access to the real estate database through a variety of computer sources:

- *CD-ROM*—One CD-ROM disk contains the entire RTC real estate inventory and has a sorting capability that allows the user to view targeted assets based on a number of investment criteria. To read and sort the data, the user must have the specialized equipment designed for these compact disks.
- *On-line access*—For those who wish to access the RTC real estate inventory via computer modem, the RTC has contracted with a service that allows the user to sort and view the data, produce a hard copy on his or her printer, and download the data to his or her personal computer.
- *Floppy disk*—The entire RTC real estate inventory data are available on floppy disks. Application software is needed for sorting and reporting the property information.

- *Magnetic tape* (nine-track, EBCDIC format)—The RTC offers the sophisticated computer user data on magnetic tape. The data are provided in a fixed format, and the user can load the data into an existing application.
- *Asset Specific Inquiry Program*—This service is designed to provide individual property reports to investors based on specific investment criteria, such as property type, state, and city. To purchase this program, call (800) RTC-3006.

These products are updated monthly for more accurate and timely information. To obtain additional information on the first four products, call (800) RTC-2990 and request a brochure about the program(s) that best meet your investment needs.

Conservatorship vs. Receivership Assets

When a savings and loan institution is determined to be insolvent, it is placed under the control of the RTC and becomes a "conservatorship institution." Once a conservatorship institution is sold and/or liquidated, any assets that are not transferred to the acquiring institution are placed into "receivership." Conservatorship and receivership assets are both under the jurisdiction of the RTC.

Properties of S&Ls in conservatorship are sold directly by the institution as REO, while properties sold from receivership are sold directly by a regional or local sales center office of the RTC. The RTC publication for residential inventory contains properties from both receiverships and conservatorships.

Dealing with the RTC

Foreclosed properties, especially bailout properties offered at auction, are being liquidated in a very competitive marketplace. To succeed at this specialized endeavor, you must first become knowledgeable and learn to compete, then you have to get good at it. If you think someone is going to gift wrap a bargain-priced home with a tag reading "Special Delivery from Uncle Sam," think again. It is you alone who must determine whether a property is a worthwhile investment.

To become knowledgeable and overcome the lack-of-experience handicap of the first-time buyer, read this book thoroughly, paying special attention to the key guidelines listed in Chapter 3. To those essential guidelines, add the following tactic, which is relevant to dealing with the RTC inventory.

As of this writing, if a property has been on the market for four months, official RTC policy allows its local supervisors to accept 20 percent less than its appraised value. But the RTC does not want to manage billions of dollars in assets—it wants to sell these properties. And to encourage this endeavor, its policy is very likely to change so that the RTC will accept even lower bids.

Using the tactic of the bargain countdown, you select a potential worthwhile property, estimate its market value, estimate the cost to renovate it, determine the price you want to buy it at, prearrange approval for financing, get to know whoever is supervising the sale (a helpful agent can keep you informed of sales activity and when other offers are being made), and then wait.

You do *not* make an offer at this time. Instead, you patiently keep track of how long the property has been on the market and make your first low offer one day before the notification of price reduction. This way you're in the ball game, so to say, and your bid has a good chance of being the winning one, even if that price reduction is big enough to encourage many buyers. Remember that the RTC is a very motivated seller, and if you make an offer that's equivalent to the price reduction with a written contract and the financing prearranged, the chances of having your offer accepted are excellent. Bear in mind also that you can use the bargain countdown tactic on more than one property at a time.

HUD Property

When mortgage lenders foreclose on a house secured with an FHA-insured mortgage, they file a claim with FHA to have the Department of Housing and Urban Development (HUD) pay the balance due on the loan and assume ownership of the foreclosed property. These properties are then put up for sale as HUD homes.

Types of HUD property available include single-family houses, condominiums, townhomes, and two- to four-unit properties. Like most other foreclosed property, all HUD properties are sold as-is—in their present condition, without any seller warranties.

HUD lists its properties for sale with certain licensed real estate brokers, called Area Management Brokers. They have a master key available, should you decide to inspect a particular HUD property.

HUD itself does not offer financing directly to home buyers, but many HUD properties qualify for FHA-insured loans, which require only a 3 percent down payment, sometimes less. If the property needs extensive renovation, HUD offers a special FHA-insured financing package that includes money for improvements. Also, HUD may pay many of your closing costs. If you get financing elsewhere, the terms are all cash to HUD in sixty days, with no contingency for financing.

The listing price of each property is HUD's estimate of fair market value. However, HUD will often accept offers for less than the listing price.

Auctions

Besides auction-type foreclosure sales, private sellers, such as
builders and developers of large housing projects, often hire
auctioneers to stimulate a sense of time pressure when a
market is so stagnant that no pressure exists. The purpose of
holding an auction is to quickly sell off surplus inventory that
might otherwise go unsold during slow or stagnant market
activity. Sometimes the hype and competitive bidding in a
closed arena will actually earn more money, and faster, than
the property could possibly earn on the open market. (The
formation of the RTC to sell off the huge inventory of the
defunct thrifts is a good example.)

Besides the usual sellers of foreclosed or surplus property,
here's a sampling of other entities that periodically auction off
their holdings:

- Municipal, county, and state governments in order to
  reduce surplus property acquired through nonpayment
  of taxes or abandonment
- The U.S. Treasury in order to liquidate property seized
  from drug dealers or other criminal offenders
- Healthy banks or S&Ls that have to liquidate property
  taken back through foreclosure
- Mortgage companies, such as the Federal National
  Mortgage Association (Fannie Mae), that have to
  liquidate holdings taken back through foreclosure

It really doesn't matter who the seller is, because the principles and procedures of buying at auction are basically the
same nationwide. Chapter 6 discusses auctions, including how
they work and how to purchase bargain-priced property while
attending them.

~ 6 ~

Buying at Auctions

In November 1990, the RTC scheduled its first-ever auction at an exclusive Miami hotel to sell off some of its troubled higher-priced properties. Over $320 million in income-producing properties were up for bid, each valued at $1 million or more. The bidders wouldn't have to be physically present, because the entire auction, including an elaborate photo and video presentation, was to be broadcast live to prospective investors in London, Tokyo, and ten major cities across the United States.

But for whatever reason, the auction never took place. Meanwhile, a new auction site is being discussed as unsold properties continue to accumulate on the RTC's vast list of inventory. When the first international auction of million-dollar-plus properties does take place, prospective bidders will be required to have on hand a deposit of anywhere from $30,000 to $500,000, depending upon the type of property that they plan to bid on. And that amount merely represents the initial deposit toward the earnest money!

Nevertheless, don't be put off by thinking these auctions are out of your league. Before the bailout is over, the RTC plans to hold a good many auctions in price ranges almost anyone can afford. In fact, the RTC is now considering a structured auction process to expedite the sale of affordable single-family and multifamily property.

HOW AUCTIONS WORK

Historically auctions were typically conducted in a circuslike atmosphere, under a tent with a fast-talking auctioneer standing on a platform, holding a gavel, and shouting off numbers that only someone with a trained ear could understand. Today's real estate auctions are a little more sophisticated. They're usually held in spacious auditoriums or hotel convention rooms with plenty of helpful visual aids.

Each participant receives a placard (a paddle) with his or her assigned number printed on it. To make a bid, the participant simply raises the numbered placard, which the auctioneer acknowledges. The auction begins with the auctioneer asking for bids, calling out each bid made, and asking for more. Once the highest bid is attained on a particular property, auction company staff will note the buyer's number and confirm his or her name and the description of the property that has just been purchased.

During the bidding, assistants, or "ring men," roam the audience, apparently with the purpose of helping the auctioneer identify bids. Very often, however, they also stimulate bidding. For instance, say you already made a bid, but someone else has momentarily outbid you. An assistant might look you right in the eye and say something like "Are you going to lose this great bargain over a few hundred dollars?" or "That property is still underpriced—can't you beat that last bid?"

Adding to the hype, successful bidders are sometimes identified with some sort of a stick-on Winner button. Regardless of how they are singled out, before leaving the auction premises, they are required to hand over deposit moneys and sign purchase contracts.

Special Formats

Real estate auctions are conducted under different types of formats, all of which revolve around the "minimum bid" accepted by the seller.

Under the *absolute auction* format, there is no minimum bid, and the seller accepts the highest bid offered, regardless of price. Most experienced auction buyers agree that more bargains, as well as more participants, are found at absolute auctions. On the other hand, if the bidding process becomes frenzied, due to the large number of participants bidding on bargain-priced offerings with no minimum bid, the result could boost prices far above expectations on a prearranged minimum.

Another variation in auction format is the *absolute auction with a minimum bid*. This format allows the seller to set a price (the minimum acceptable bid) below which anything is unacceptable. Bidding will usually begin at the minimum bid price. Should the auctioned property receive a minimum bid or higher, it will be sold the same day.

Under a *reserve auction* format, the seller reserves the right to accept or reject the highest bid of the day. The seller typically confirms the sale within forty-eight hours. This, of course, means that the successful bidder will have to wait until confirmation before knowing whether or not he or she actually purchased a property. Due to its, excuse the pun, "reservations," the reserve auction format is not very popular among auction participants and is seldom used.

The most popular type of auction used today is a blend of other formats called the *mixed auction*. Here the auctioneer mixes absolute auction property with reserve auction property. As an example, a developer, knowing that absolute auctions bring the most participants, would advertise No Minimum Bid—Property Will Be Sold to Highest Bidder, and in fact would auction off a *limited* number of units at whatever price they might bring. However, the remaining units will be auctioned with a reserve. In other words, the seller reserves the right to say "No sale" on the remaining units if the bids are considered unacceptable.

Another format is the *pooled-unit auction*, primarily used by developers when available units are similar in style and size and are within one complex, such as co-op apartments or a condominium community. Under this format, the available units are grouped together, and participants are bidding to buy one unit among the pooled group. The highest bidder gets first choice among the units in the pool. The next highest bidder gets second choice, and so on. One variation in this format allows the bidding to begin again in a second round, with the winning bidder getting first choice from the remaining units.

Bidding Requirements

Start by obtaining information about the auction, such as a brochure or prospectus on the available property. You can do this by visiting the on-site auction office or by calling the developer, lender, or auctioneer holding the sale. The brochure will include information about available financing (if any), registration procedures, minimum bid requirements, property information, and earnest-money requirements.

Admission is usually limited to preregistered participants and their guests. It is also likely you'll have to present a cashier's check for $2,500, $5,000, or more in order to be admitted. If you're not successful at bidding, you can simply deposit the cashier's check in your bank account the next day.

If you make the winning bid and your offer is accepted, you are technically committed to completing the purchase. If you decide to back out of the deal for whatever reason (such as cold feet or buyer's remorse), the auctioneer can, in most cases, legally keep your cashier's check.

Backing out of a deal can have even more detrimental results. Some auctioneers will demand that you purchase the property even if you later fail to arrange the financing needed to complete the deal. So, if you fail to arrange financing, you'll not only lose your deposit but may also be forced to go through with the deal.

Financing On-Site

It is true that auction buyers who come to the arena fully prepared most often pick up the best deals. But participants often overlook one of the most important factors involved in buying at auction: the prearranged financing to close the deal.

Do not underestimate the importance of good financing. Most often it can mean the difference between a marginal bargain and a great bargain.

Some auctions offer on-site financing. This can occur when the seller, such as a builder or developer, made arrangements to offer financing to buyers. This "on-site lender" is often a mortgage broker—meaning that he or she can offer loans that are funded by several financial institutions.

A thriving S&L that sells its foreclosed property at auction will sometimes offer financing to buyers. When it does, the S&L is said to make a *loan to facilitate*. When the seller is also the lender, which is always the case in a loan to facilitate, it's often possible to negotiate advantageous loan terms. You can save in interest charges, points, incidental escrow fees, and the amount of down payment required.

GUIDELINES FOR PROFITABLE AUCTION BUYING

Do you know the two greatest pitfalls associated with investing in real estate? They are *overpaying* and *not knowing exactly what you're getting.* These pitfalls are especially perilous at auctions, primarily because there is competitive bidding (which promotes a sense of urgency among buyers) and most property is sold as-is (with no warranties by the seller as to the condition of the property). But these inherent dangers are easy to overcome with a little study and effort.

All successful auction investors, the men and women who make the best deals, have learned certain abilities that put them head and shoulders above the rest. Essentially, these abilities revolve around two important factors: *knowledge* and *preparation*. Investors who avoid the pitfalls and bid success-fully are typically the ones who spend the time doing all the necessary preparatory work before the auction. They arrive at the auction arena fully prepared, armed with the knowledge needed to compete and do business profitably.

Following are eight specific guidelines that will help to minimize risk and make you a successful auction investor.

Have Knowledge of Value

Having knowledge of local property values, as already men-tioned in Chapter 3, is the most important factor in all real estate dealings. Without accurately determining value, you risk the danger of paying too much for a particular investment, which will cut into your profit or, even worse, lead to financial loss.

Knowledge of local property values not only saves you money, it makes you more efficient as well. If, for instance, you see an auction advertised with a minimum bid and your research leads you to believe that the difference between the minimum and market value is too slight, you might as well stay home.

Generally speaking, you should use all the guidelines men-tioned in Chapter 3 to select a worthwhile auction-eligible investment. But if you're still uncertain of value, don't be afraid to pay for a professional appraisal. The few hundred dollars that it costs could save you several thousand.

Avoid Impulsive Buying

Quite often some auction buyers are caught up in all the hype and activity and make the mistake of bidding emotionally. After all, it takes only a moment to raise a paddle. And it's only natural sometimes to act on impulse, especially with so much going on to stimulate the participants: the fast-talking auctioneer, ring men encouraging the bidders, competition from the other bidders, and the sense of immediacy (it's now or never). But the well-informed and prepared auction buyer uses rational restraint, knowing that other auctions will be held and this is *not* the only chance for a great bargain.

Choose Several Properties

Unless you're interested in one particular property and intend to buy that specific property only, it's advantageous to list several appealing investments. Your chances for picking up a super bargain are greater when there's more than one acceptable property to bid on. Not only that, it will help to keep your emotions at a manageable level when other bidders are chasing your first selection.

Make Thorough Inspections

Remember that most foreclosed property is sold as-is, and that once you have signed the purchase contract it's too late to negotiate over anything in disrepair—a sagging roof, malfunctioning plumbing, or the crumbling foundation, for example. A professional inspection serves a number of purposes. First, it

will bring to your attention any problems and items in disrepair, and thereby help you determine whether or not the
property is a worthwhile investment. Second, it will assist you
in estimating the renovation costs, which must be calculated
into the price you're willing to pay. Finally, it assists you in
projecting the probable life expectancy of the structural components and working systems of the property.

Remember the old saying "It takes money to make money"?
When it comes to property inspections, this proverb is especially true. But you might say, "At about $250 per inspec-
tion—and there are six properties that interest me—that will
cost me $1,500!" That's right, and buying at auction should
save you at least ten times that amount off the market value of
each property you purchase! (You'll find more information
about property inspections in Chapter 7.)

Determine Your Maximum-Bid Price

Although the maximum-bid price is calculated the same way,
it is more important than the maximum-offer price, because
you'll be bidding at an auction, not negotiating (making written offers or counteroffers over an extended period) in the
open market. In other words, time is of the essence, especially
when bidding at auction. You have to determine an absolute
maximum price prior to the auction, then resolve not to
exceed it, no matter what.

The calculation for figuring the max-bid price is identical to
that of figuring the max-offer price, which you read about in
Chapter 3. For your convenience, it's repeated here. First
estimate the costs to renovate the property, then calculate
your bargain so that your maximum-bid purchase price plus
your estimated renovation costs is 25 percent below the
market value of similar real estate. Therefore, if you deduct 25
percent from the market value of a comparable property in

move-in condition worth $160,000, you get $120,000. From this figure you deduct the estimated cost of renovations—in this case, $8,000—and the result is a max-bid price of $112,000.

Compile Maximum-Bid Cards

A maximum-bid card is a 3″ × 5″ index card that serves as a ready reference about the property you're interested in. On the top line, identify the property. On the next line, print your max-bid price (the highest amount you're willing to pay for auction-eligible property). Below the max-bid price, print your opinion of probable existing market value. Note that the market value figure should be substantially *higher* than your max-bid price. When figuring the probable market value, ask yourself, "If I buy this property today at this price, and sell it tomorrow, can I at least break even?" The answer should be yes. Your goal is to buy far enough below the market value that if you sold the property immediately, you would not lose any money.

To help you identify the property, a more detailed max-bid card could include a photograph of the property with listed plus and minus features about the unit.

Keep these reference cards with you at the auction, and refer to them often. Remember not to exceed your established max-bid price.

Prearrange Financing

Most auction sales *do not allow* a contingency for obtaining financing. If this is the case, then you must either have the full sales price in cash or take enough cash or a cashier's check for a deposit and arrange financing for the balance owing before the auction. Otherwise, without adequate funding, you lose the normal 10 percent earnest-money deposit!

Although some auctions will offer on-site financing, do some checking around. Talk with mortgage lenders or mortgage brokers to see how much you can borrow and where to get the best rates. It's the only way to tell if the on-site financing being offered is reasonable or just a rip-off. (More information about how to get financing appears in Chapters 4 and 5.)

Examine All Pertinent Documents

As you probably already have surmised (especially from the guidelines in Chapter 3), I'm a big proponent of investing in single-family houses. And for several already-mentioned reasons, I am not in favor of condominium or co-op ownership. However, if you plan to invest in such a unit, please be aware of certain restrictions that pertain to use of the property. These "by-laws" or "house rules," often referred to as CC&Rs (covenants, conditions, and restrictions), are the homeowners' association's provisions the owner must abide by. Get a copy of such provisions and read them carefully, paying special attention to limitations on rentals, age, pets, number of vehicles, and children. Be certain you can live with them, because they're very difficult to change.

In addition, be sure to check the association's financial condition before purchasing a unit. Beware of an insolvent association. Later on you may be levied with a special assessment to make the association solvent.

When considering the purchase of occupied rental property, ask to look over the record books. Pay special attention to rent receipts, taxes, insurance premiums, and maintenance costs of the last year.

If you are considering the purchase of a single-family house, get information on taxes, assessments (sewer and street), water, waste removal, and the costs and restrictions (if any) of belonging to so-called neighborhood associations.

Last but not least is the always crucial purchase contract. Keep in mind that the purchase of real property will likely be the most expensive investment you ever make. And the purchase contract that legally binds you, the buyer, to its terms should *not* be entered into casually. To protect yourself, before the sale get a copy of the purchase contract that will be used at the auction. Read it over carefully, and if you have any questions or doubts about it, discuss it with a capable attorney who specializes in real estate. If your attorney believes certain changes are necessary, ask the auctioneer or whoever is handling the property to arrange them before the sale.

AUCTION MISCELLANY

Shills

Did you know that some unscrupulous auctioneers insert "shills" (often called straw men) into the audience to induce honest buyers to bid higher? In the gambling meccas throughout the world, a shill is someone who works for the house and is inserted into the game—a poker or crap game, for example—for the purpose of keeping it alive. In the auction arena their purpose is similar—to keep the bidding alive. They'll often bid whenever there's a quiet moment to force honest buyers to bid higher for the properties they want. And you'll see them become silent whenever the action gets hot.

If you witness such behavior, especially when the same person never makes a winning bid, you have probably spotted a shill. If this is the case and you suspect that one or more are inflating the bidding, just leave. You're up against a no-win situation, and your time is better spent elsewhere.

Rescission Laws

Certain states have consumer *rescission laws* that allow buyers to nullify a contract sale within a specified period of time. No explanation is required of the buyer for the change of mind. States that have such legislation allow the buyer to nullify the sale if he or she notifies the seller in writing within a certain period (usually three to fourteen days) after signing a contract. Phone the real estate commissioner's office to find out whether such consumer protection laws exist in your state.

Right of First Refusal

Do you know about the *right of first refusal*? If, for example, you're outbid on a particular property during the auction sale, you still have a chance to buy it. People do change their minds (remember the rescission laws), and mistakes do occur. After the auction is concluded, tell a member of the auction staff that you would like a right of first refusal on the property. It gives you the right to buy the property *under the same terms as the successful bidder*, should he or she, for whatever reason, not buy the property.

HOW TO FIND AUCTIONS

Developers, lenders, and government agencies typically advertise auctions in local newspapers. You can get information from the RTC about its inventory and upcoming auctions by calling the Assets for Sale number: (800) 431-0600.

In most cases, the lenders, developers, the RTC, and other government agencies use private auctioneers to conduct their auctions. You can obtain the names of auctioneers in your area by calling the National Auctioneers Association at (913) 541-8084. Once you know the auction companies that are operating in your area, call them individually and ask to be placed on their mailing lists.

For information about auction-eligible property seized by

law enforcement agencies, write to either the U.S. Customs Office or the National Asset Seizure and Forfeiture (NASAF) Office of the U.S. Marshal's Service. You can write the Customs Office at:

U.S. Customs Office
P.O. Box 17423
Gateway I Bldg.
Washington, DC 20041

You can write to the NASAF at one of its regional offices:

880 Front St.
1-S-1 Federal Bldg.
San Diego, CA 92188

1258 Federal Bldg.
300 N. Los Angeles St.
Los Angeles, CA 90012

Room 465 Federal Bldg.
1961 Stout St.
Denver, CO 80294

2104 U.S. Courthouse
515 Rusk Ave.
Houston, TX 77002

210 Building, Room 1171
210 N. Tucker
St. Louis, MO 63101

1416 J. W. McCormick and
Courthouse Bldg.
P.O. Box 1146, Room 407
230 S. Dearborn
Chicago, IL 60604

231 W. Lafayette St.
645 Federal Bldg./
Courthouse
P.O. Box 2869
Detroit, MI 48231

Federal Building Annex
77 Forsyth St. SW, 1st
Mezzanine
Atlanta, GA 30303

606 U.S. Courthouse
101 W. Lombard St.
Baltimore, MD 21201

244 U.S. Courthouse
300 N.E. 1st Ave.
Miami, FL 33132

~ 7 ~

Appraisal: How Much Is the Property Worth?

Once upon a time in a wonderful place, a three-bedroom house cost $14,000. The interest rate on the mortgage to buy that house was 5 percent—and all you needed was a job and a down payment of $860 to move in. For about $2,700 you could own a new Chevy Impala, a first-run movie was only $1.50, a candy bar cost a mere nickel, and a six-pack of beer cost less than a dollar.

This inexpensive-sounding place was, of course, the United States. And the time was not so long ago: 1967. Back in 1967 nobody had ever heard of an adjustable-rate mortgage or a kitchen with a built-in microwave oven. And the idea of condominium-type ownership had not yet been contrived.

Times change. The house that cost $14,000 in 1967 is worth $150,000 today, and the $860 down payment back then wouldn't even pay this year's property taxes. But although many changes have occurred over the years in types of ownership and in the forms of financing being offered, the principles of making a profit never change.

MARKET VALUE

To succeed in this ever-changing industry, you must understand and adhere to its tried, proven, and enduring principles. Inevitably, most of those principles revolve around the meaning of value or, more precisely, *market value*.

What exactly is market value? Most professionals—the mortgage lenders, real estate salespeople, and savvy investors—would say it's the highest price an informed and willing buyer will pay and the lowest price an informed and able seller will accept. If three professional appraisers evaluated the same property, they would arrive at three different opinions of value. However, the variation would likely be slight; each opinion would be in a certain range of value of what the subject property would be expected to sell at.

Yet for the profit-minded investor, market value has to have more meaning than educated opinions or an industry-accepted definition that designates the amount of money exchanged between buyer and seller. To properly evaluate market value, your analysis must include other important factors—supply and demand, location, condition, and cash flow. Just as important, and often overlooked, an appraisal of an investment property's market value should include its expectation to earn a profit.

To succeed in the business of distressed-property investing, you must first learn how to spot a good investment property. You must master that skill, coordinated with learning how to acquire it at the least possible cost and with the best possible terms, then using several proven tactics to make it profitable. This chapter provides property evaluation information that will enable you to spot a diamond in the rough. You will need the remainder of the book, however, to complete your mastery of the overall course in how to make a profit in distressed property.

SUPPLY AND DEMAND

If you could somehow look into the future, it goes without saying that you'd be rich. You'd know where demand will be before it gets there. For example, knowing that a huge regional shopping center was going to be built on a specific site, you could buy that land and make a tremendous profit when you sold out to the shopping center developer.

But in reality we don't have crystal balls that reveal the future. We have to rely on instinct and observation of current happenings in order to anticipate where demand will be. But there's another factor. We also have to know *what* will be in demand. Land oversteps the "what" question because, under favorable zoning laws, land is available for whatever purpose that's required. However, when you're buying buildings, you're investing in function. Your building could be in the midst of the highest-demand area in the city, but if no one wants what you have, it will remain a poor investment.

What's Hot and What's Not

You probably remember the "condomania" that erupted in the mid-1970s and peaked in the late 1980s. The condominium style of ownership—an apartmentlike unit with common-area amenities and without the burden of lawn care by the owner— became somewhat popular during this period. Developers erected condos because they not only made a profit on them, but they could also build eight condo units on the same amount of land that it took to build one single-family house. And speculators found they could, with a few minor changes, make a profit by converting an entire apartment complex into condominiums and selling off the individual units.

Today condos are so overbuilt in most regions of the country that values are either stagnant or falling. Now there is less demand than supply, and with little exception, many of the people who are buying condos are doing so because they can't afford anything else.

Surveys reveal that today's first-time home buyers really want a moderately priced house with three bedrooms, two baths, a garage, and their own piece of earth. (In Chapter 9, you'll find more information on what today's home buyers really want.)

As you can see, by using hindsight, it's easy to reflect on what was overbuilt in the past and what's currently in demand. But how do you know what will be in demand, say, in the next year or five years from now? And how do you know what will be overbuilt?

The answer is part of something mentioned earlier: you have to rely on instinct and observation of current happenings in order to anticipate where demand will be. Of course, you can do this more efficiently by observing the events that affect real estate values in your own area. This is the primary reason you should invest locally.

Supply and Demand Facts

Since properties in demand always bring better prices and demand for different types of property is directly related to population growth and events occurring in your area, the following facts should be helpful in what to watch for:

- Is the area you plan to invest in thriving or declining? Your objective is to invest in thriving areas that are

economically sound, are growing in population, and
have the potential for resale profit. You want to avoid
areas that are declining in population, or are becoming
blighted, and have no potential for resale profit.

- Are new transportation facilities proposed or being
  built? As a positive indicator of future growth and real
  estate demand, watch for new highways, especially
  proposed interchanges that will enhance the value of
  nearby commercial property. Other indicators of growth
  are new airports or a significant increase in activity at
  existing ones.

- Are major corporate facilities locating in your area?
  When big companies build office space or a production
  plant in an area, the demand for housing and services is
  going to increase. The reverse is also true. If big
  business decides to pull out, real estate values will fall.

- On the supply side of the equation, remember that too
  much of anything means lower prices. Look for property
  in your area that's in short supply now and for property
  you expect to be in short supply two, three, or five
  years from now. To give you a clue as to what's
  currently overbuilt and what's in short supply, check on
  vacancy rates for particular types of housing with your
  local board of Realtors. To determine the future supply
  (what's being built now and proposed construction) of a
  particular type of housing, you can attend meetings of
  the planning board and talk with real estate agents. Be
  aware that what's most popular now, whatever type of
  extensive construction being built, will likely mean an
  oversupply of those particular units in two to five years.
  This, of course, also means that those types of units
  will *not* be a good investment.

WHAT'S A GOOD DEAL?

As you can see, you must consider supply and demand factors when determining the quality of a potential investment. Yet the primary factor in whether or not the property is a bargain still depends on its price in relation to market value. Obviously, the further below market value you buy property, the better the bargain.

Methods of determining market value in real estate vary according to the type of property you're buying. The following guidelines are for doing a quick and accurate appraisal of single-family and multifamily residential property.

Single-Family Residential Property

As mentioned before, if you can buy foreclosed single-family houses at 15 percent below the current going rate for similar property, that's usually a good deal. But if the property is run-down and requires considerable money and/or time to be made salable, you must figure what's a bargain differently. First estimate the costs to renovate the property, then calculate your bargain so that your maximum-offer purchase price plus your estimated renovation costs is 25 percent below the market value of similar real estate.

But you might ask, "Why does my maximum-offer purchase price have to be so far below market value?" It's because renovations on a fixer-upper will likely cost more and take longer than you estimate. And you may have several reasons for investing in real estate, but your primary objective should be to earn a profit at this venture. To this end, you want your purchase price to give you some assurance that a profit is fairly certain.

Many factors are involved in determining value: amenities,

condition, location. Yet they all have a common denominator: the price per square foot. It's the most important factor in quickly determining market value of nonincome-producing residential real estate.

For example, if a home is selling for $100,000 and has 2,000 square feet of living space, simply divide the selling price by the square footage. The result is the cost per square foot. In this instance, the price per square foot is $50. From this example, if you already know that comparable homes in a particular neighborhood are selling for $50 per square foot, then you can be assured that if you purchase a home for $40 per square foot or less, you will have most likely made a good buy.

Comparable Sales Method

The comparable sales method of appraisal compares the property you are interested in with similar properties that have recently sold in the same area. A simple application of the comparable sales method compares the subject property—the one you want to appraise—with three similar properties that have recently sold, are located within the same area, and basically have no meaningful differences. These other properties are known as "comparables."

For instance, say all three comparables sold at a price ranging from $80,000 to $82,000. They had the same square footage of living area and lot size. The subject property is similar in quality of construction and lot size; however, it has a 300-square-foot den and a swimming pool, which the comparables do not have. Therefore, based on this information, the subject property is worth $81,000 (the midpoint of the range) plus the value of a den and swimming pool.

When you determine the value of the den and swimming pool, then you'll have the approximate appraised value of the subject. The den is 300 square feet, and building it today would cost about $40 per square foot, or $12,000. You also determine that a comparable swimming pool costs $10,000. So your final estimate of value would be $81,000 plus $22,000 for the den and pool, or a total appraised value of $103,000.

Use the Market Analysis Form in Table 7.1 on page 90 for noting important data on comparables that will help you make your final evaluation. When comparing the subject property with the comparables, remember that you have to adjust the price of the comparables by adding or subtracting the value of amenities to arrive at an estimate of value. For instance, if a comparable has one bedroom more than the subject property, you must subtract the value of that bedroom from the comparable. If a comparable does not have a garage and the subject property does, then you must add the value of the garage to the comparable in order to arrive at a reconciled (adjusted) value for the subject property.

This, of course, is an oversimplification of evaluating the worth of a property. Yet it takes into consideration important factors in doing a quick and simple appraisal.

Getting to Know the Market

Before you can make an accurate appraisal, you have to know the market where you plan to invest. It's not only essential to know the prices properties have sold for, but you should also be informed of asking prices.

You learn the market by doing your homework. Start by obtaining from a Realtor an MLS (multiple-listing service) book, and get a feel for what's available. Inquire into asking prices in your neighborhood. Also look up recent sales of similar properties (comparables) in the back of the MLS book, what vacant lots sell for, and especially take note of the price per square foot. The most important factor in determining value of improved property is price per square foot.

From your research, determine the range that property in your area sells for at price per square foot. From this informa-

TABLE 7.1 MARKET ANALYSIS FORM

Subject Property Address: _____ Date: _____

Information on similar properties in same general area that may have the same approximate value:

Currently for Sale

Address	Bedrooms	Baths	Den/Fam. Rm.	Sq. Ft.	Price/Sq. Ft.	Mortgages	Interest Rate	Days on Market

Sold Within Last Six Months

Address	Bedrooms	Baths	Den/Fam. Rm.	Sq. Ft.	Price/Sq. Ft.	Mortgages	Interest Rate	Days on Market

Note: Realtors and old MLS books can be helpful for finding past sale information.

tion alone, you can usually determine quickly whether a property deserves further attention. You want to investigate a property only if it is likely to sell for more per square foot than you paid for it.

Try thinking like a house builder. If a builder can buy a vacant lot for $10,000 and build a 1,000-square-foot house for $40,000 at $40 per square foot, the total cost is $50,000. If the builder sells the house for $60,000, or $50 per square foot plus the cost of the land, the profit will be $10,000.

Also become familiar with local values by checking out open houses on weekends and reading through local real estate want ads.

The greatest risk of investing in real estate is paying too much for it. You can avoid this inherent pitfall by carefully analyzing the market before you invest. Well-informed investors know a bargain when they see one and, conversely, are fully aware if a property is overpriced.

Multifamily Residential Property

The category of housing known as multifamily residential property includes everything from duplexes to apartment buildings. These types of properties are considered income property, so the primary factor in their evaluation is the amount of income they earn.

Appraisal by Gross Income Multiplier

A quick and simple method of determining an approximate value of a property with respect to its gross income (income before expenses) is to use a gross income multiplier. This method cannot be classed as a professional approach, yet investors often use it as a quick, off-the-cuff calculation to determine whether a property deserves further attention.

Often, in newspaper ads for income properties, you'll see a sales price given as "eight times the gross." This means that the sales price of that particular property is eight times the current gross income. For example, if the property is grossing $20,000, then the selling price would be that figure times 8, or $160,000. In this case, 8 is the gross income multiplier.

As with the capitalization rate (which you'll read about next), the gross income multiplier is determined by the appraiser within a range of values, considering the "going rate" for the area. This going rate is normally between 4 and 12, where the lower number represents the less desirable locations. Thus, for properties with a gross income of $20,000 per year, this might be the range of values:

Location	Multiplier	Value
Worst area	4	$80,000
Average area	7	$140,000
Best area	11	$220,000

The gross income multiplier only gives you a ballpark estimate. It does not reflect the effects of operating expenses, and it's unreliable for arriving at true market value.

Appraisal by Capitalization

Also referred to as the income approach to appraisal, the capitalization method is more exact, taking into consideration all the pertinent expenses relevant to the property in order to arrive at fair market value. Table 7.2 lists the type of income and expense information that will assist you at evaluation under the capitalization method.

Note that the property in this example earned gross equity income of $14,600, but because of depreciation, it actually showed a taxable loss of $7,024. This illustrates the tax shelter benefit of owning income-producing real estate.

TABLE 7.2 INCOME PROPERTY STATEMENT

Description: 18-unit apartment building, all 2-bedroom units, each renting at $600 monthly

1. **Gross annual income** (100% occupancy)		$129,600
2. Vacancies and collection loss (5%)	$ 6,480	
3. Annual operating expenses		
4. Trash removal	13,000	
5. Property taxes	14,200	
6. Insurance	4,200	
7. Utilities	3,100	
8. Advertising	360	
9. Resident manager	7,200	
10. Supplies	240	
11. Reserve for replacement and repairs (5% of line 1)	6,480	
12. Total operating expenses, including vacancy and collection loss		(55,260)
13. **Net operating income** (line 1 − line 12)		$74,340
14. Loan payments (P&I)		(64,000)
15. **Gross spendable income** (line 13 − line 14)		$10,340
16. Principal payment (equity buildup)		4,260
17. **Gross equity income** (line 15 + line 16)		$14,600
18. Depreciation		(21,624)
19. **Taxable income** (line 17 − line 18)		$(7,024)

The net operating income represents what the property would earn if purchased for cash, free and clear of any loans. To determine *capitalized* value, the appraiser compares this amount to the rate of return he or she would expect to receive on such an investment. The appraiser divides net operating income by this capitalization rate, usually in the range of 8 to 12 percent. The appraiser expects the greatest returns on the riskiest investments, so the cap rate depends on the risk of investment, measured by such characteristics as the type of property and the quality of its income. Prime oceanfront property, for example, would be capitalized in the lower range because it carries less risk and greater potential for price appreciation. Property capitalized in the higher range might include inner-city units located in a blighted slum or high-crime area.

To use this approach with the property analyzed in Table 7.2, apply a midrange cap rate of 10 percent, assuming the property is average. Dividing the net operating income of $74,340 by 10 percent results in a capitalized estimate of fair market value of $743,400. If the property was considered prime, we'd divide the net operating income by 8 percent and attain an estimated value of $929,250. Conversely, if we apply a cap rate of 12 percent, the estimate of value is $619,500. As you can see, this means you'd pay the least for the riskiest investments.

INSPECTING THE PROPERTY

Once you've taken title to a property, you can see your profits evaporate if you discover a major structural problem or a myriad of other needed repairs. Therefore, property inspection is a key to success when investing in real estate. This is especially true when you're investing in distressed property, which is commonly sold without any warranties from the seller.

For you to profit at investing in any particular property, you or someone you hire must be able to accurately estimate the cost of the renovations needed to make the property habitable or salable. Unless you're capable of efficiently and effectively inspecting a property—one that very likely needs moderate or extensive renovation—you're better off hiring someone who is.

Hiring a Professional

A professional inspection is a detailed evaluation of the condition of the property, including its structural elements and working systems. It is nothing else—not an appraisal or an opinion of whether or not you're making a good buy. You must decide, using the information provided by the property inspector, whether the property is a good deal.

Having a professional inspection of the property serves three purposes. First, it will point out any major problems, thereby helping you to decide whether or not the property is worth buying. Second, it will help you to estimate the renovation costs. Third, the inspection will help you to determine the probable life expectancy of the working systems and structural elements of the property. If you're buying apartment units, this information will be helpful in allocating reserve capital for future expenses and projecting cash flow.

You can expect to pay about $250 to $350, on average, for a professional inspection of a house. Fees to inspect commercial or large multiunit properties are typically higher. Consider this a necessary cost of doing business—an insurance policy of sorts, protection against making the mistake of buying a costly, malfunctioning lemon of a property.

A good inspection is worth many, many times the fee paid. Too much is at stake to make such a major investment without accurately knowing exactly what you're getting. Furthermore, you need an unbiased opinion from an expert to help keep your investment decision a good one. A professional inspector has nothing to gain by giving you a false perspective. On the other hand, buyers often get emotionally involved with a particular property (some have to have it no matter what the cost or condition) and become irrational.

Here are a few facts to help convince you that professional help at property inspection is absolutely essential:

- Most foreclosed property is sold in as-is condition, meaning the buyer gets what's there and nothing else. The seller, whether it's the RTC or a thriving S&L, makes no warranties or promises whatsoever as to the property's condition. The foundation could be buckling, the floor joists could be rotting, and certain renovations might not be up to code. Once you take title to the property, the problems are all yours.
- Old houses can change ownership and continue in use regardless of the fact they are not up to current building codes. This means the houses were "grandfathered" because they existed before the codes were written. If you purchased one of these old houses with the intention of making renovations that require a building permit, you could be forced to bring the entire house up to current code. The cost could be prohibitive.
- When you convert a structure from one use to another, such as a residence to business use, you're required to meet the building codes for the new use. This code requirement could cost thousands in new sprinklers and fire alarm systems, plumbing, and parking spaces.

Choosing a Property Inspector

To choose a property inspector, start by getting recommendations from your prospective lender or friends who have recently used an inspection service. You can also use the yellow pages of the telephone book, taking special note of advertisements that mention years in business. Additionally, regarding residential property, you can call the American Society of Home Inspectors at (202) 842-3096 for a recommended firm in your area.

What to Look for from an Inspection

An accurate property inspection will not solve all your problems. But it will point out potential problem areas and help guide you in the decision-making process. Being forewarned in this business can not only save you from worrisome headaches, but will save you plenty of money as well.

Here are four solid reasons *not* to buy a particular property:

- A malfunctioning sewer or septic system
- Unsafe or insufficient water supply
- Uneven ground settling, causing structural stress or a buckling foundation
- Uncontrollable water leakage in basement walls or floor

In summary, it's a good deal when . . .

- The type of investment is right for you.
- The property, including estimated necessary repairs, can be purchased at substantially below market value.
- The property earns positive cash flow.
- Your analysis of supply and demand in the area indicates the potential for resale profit.

~ 8 ~

Negotiating and Making
an Offer

You've been combing the local area seeking a good investment, and you find one that looks promising. Now what do you do? First, before you make a formal written offer, gather all the information you can about the property and make an appraisal of it.

When inquiring about a property to invest in, you should ask the seller or the seller's agent these questions:

- How many square feet of living area are there?
- What is the lot size?
- Is existing financing assumable? If so, what is the interest rate? Is the interest rate fixed or variable? Is the existing financing a VA, FHA, or conventional loan?
- How many bedrooms and baths are there?
- Is there a garage?
- What is the down payment requirement?
- Will the seller carry a second mortgage?
- What year was the house built?
- What is the reason for selling?

Also establish the maximum dollar amount that you're willing to pay for the property (the max-offer price we talked about before). This price represents the final offer. Anything above this price is not worth paying, because it makes the property too expensive to be a bargain. The price you actually pay should be substantially below the established maximum, because then you've definitely made a good investment.

THE INITIAL OFFER

The best way to negotiate the purchase is to prepare a formal written offer. It, along with an earnest-money deposit, is submitted to the seller or the seller's agent. The offer to purchase spells out in detail the terms and conditions under which you're willing to purchase the property. Remember that it's a legally binding contract, which when accepted and signed by the seller binds you to its contents.

How much should you offer? You have already established the most you'd pay, so your first offering will be somewhere below that price, a price that will at least stimulate the buyer. It's customary to presume that the seller has likely built into the asking price a margin of price reduction to allow for negotiation. You don't want to offer full price unless you know that the seller is firm on price and that the property is such a bargain it's well worth the asking price. On the other hand, a ridiculously low offer may not be taken seriously.

Your objective, then, is to make an offer that has a reasonable chance of being accepted. If it isn't accepted, at least it should be good enough to stimulate a counteroffer from the seller. If you already know that similar homes in the area have sold at approximately the price the sellers are asking for their property, then, assuming that the list price is fairly close to market value, make an offer 10 to 15 percent below asking price.

This is only one example. Every situation is different, and

much depends on whether the seller is motivated and on market demand for similar properties.

BARGAINING

Bargaining to reach agreement is what negotiating is all about. Unless you're prepared to pay all cash, and at the seller's asking price, you'll be bargaining for price and terms. As a rule, if a seller is firm on price, then negotiate terms. If the seller is firm on terms, then negotiate price. If the seller is firm on neither, then negotiate both. If the seller is firm on both, then start looking for another investment—unless, of course, the asking price is just too good to pass up, which is unlikely.

During negotiations you want to avoid a frenzied bidding war with competitive buyers. The only party who benefits when two or more people are competing to buy a particular property is the seller. The added competition makes it too difficult to procure a good investment. Besides, why bother with competition when several other potential bargains are available from motivated sellers? You only need to locate them.

COUNTEROFFERS

Frequently the seller will find your initial offer unacceptable and in most cases will propose a counteroffer. Once a counteroffer is proposed, the initial offer is terminated.

The procedure of offer-counteroffer is important because it brings out the flexibility of buyer and seller. If you're confronted with an inflexible seller, don't waste any more of your time. Chalk up your effort and time to experience, and find another property. But if the property remains an excellent buy, then continue to pursue an agreement.

Once you have a good idea of what the seller wants out of

the property, start negotiating price. Get the price as low as you possibly can before doing anything else. You then negotiate terms. Begin bargaining on the down payment, keeping it as small as possible, since you need to preserve your cash to make renovations and other investments. Remember the principle of leverage: the less you have invested in the property, the more leverage you'll have, and the greater your return on investment will be.

EARNEST-MONEY DEPOSIT

When you submit the written offer, you will have to make an earnest-money deposit. This is a payment you make as a sign of your good faith; if the seller accepts your offer, it is nonrefundable. Any amount ranging from $500 to $3,000 would be appropriate as an earnest-money deposit on property worth less than about $200,000.

Keep your deposit minimal so as to limit your liability. Why? If you're forced, for whatever reason, to back out of the transaction, you need to keep your losses to a minimum. Should the offer be accepted, it's likely that the seller or the seller's agent will require a larger deposit to secure the transaction and protect his or her interest.

CONTINGENCY CLAUSES

You also need to protect yourself by including in your offer certain "subject to" clauses or contingencies. In particular, if you intend to originate a new first mortgage to purchase the property, your offer should be contingent on obtaining the financing. Such a clause might read, "This offer is subject to the buyer acquiring a new first mortgage in the approximate amount of $60,000, at prevailing rates and terms, within sixteen working days of acceptance of this offer." Thus, if you cannot acquire such financing, the contingency clause voids the offer, and you get your earnest-money deposit back.

Contingency clauses can cover almost anything, and you need certain ones to limit your liability. However, keep in mind that the seller or seller's agent will attempt to eliminate excessive contingencies, because they tend to complicate what would otherwise be a simple transaction.

CONCLUSION

Whatever you and the seller finally agree on, you are going to have to live with. Therefore, it's imperative that you be fully informed of comparable values and bargain for a good deal.

~ 9 ~

Profitable Renovations

Once you have purchased a distressed property that could be considered an undervalued fixer-upper, then the objective is to make the house worth thousands more with a minimum of effort and expenditure. To do this, you must treat the house as the investment it truly is. You accomplish this by adding improvements that buyers in the market deem important—not what you, individually, feel to be important. For instance, you may feel that a gazebo out in the backyard is worth $2,000. But to a potential home buyer who is *not* interested in a gazebo, it's worthless.

On the other hand, home buyers are looking for features like fireplaces, a family room, more than one bathroom, a laundry room, and patios and decks. These are amenities that today's home buyers are seeking, and they will pay for them.

To make your home worth thousands more, while at the same time earning a profit from the improvements you've made, you must upgrade according to knowledge of what potential home buyers are looking for, and give your home a certain style that appeals to the greatest amount of potential home buyers. The idea is to make simple improvements that will increase the value of your home, and increase it proportionately more than the cost of the improvements. For instance, it's possible to add desirability as well as $3,000 in value to your home simply by planting $600 in landscaping.

Once you envision your home merely as an object in the marketplace, you will see how to make it worth the most for the least expenditure.

WHAT HOME BUYERS WANT

Many homeowners make the mistake of making inappropriate improvements, ones that may satisfy their own needs but not the needs of the marketplace. You will definitely get a better price for the house if it appeals to a large number of buyers, instead of a rare individual.

Home buyers want a house that's tastefully decorated, with quality construction, in good condition, and a little different. And they will pay a premium to get these things.

According to a recent survey, home buyers want bigger houses and yards, at least two bathrooms, and an oversized master suite. Nearly 80 percent want a full basement. More than half want three bedrooms. Almost two-thirds want a separate dining room. Almost half want a two-car garage and more storage area, kitchens with eating space, larger family rooms, and larger closets. The survey also noted that porches and patios are very popular.

PLANNING IS ESSENTIAL

Making improvements to the house you buy and at the same time gaining the most value from them just doesn't happen without thoughtful planning. If you want to succeed at recouping proportionately more than what you invest in the renovations, then you must carefully plan the renovations you make.

Ideally, you want to take full advantage of the effects of inflation on your investment in renovations. You do this by planning now for the gains that will be earned later.

Put the investment odds in your favor by analyzing the overall housing marketplace, then make appropriate lowest-cost renovations that appeal to the greatest number of buyers. By shrewdly planning improvements, you can be assured that, over the long term, you will earn an outstanding rate of return on your renovation investment. This is primarily due to inflation and satisfaction of the buyer's demand in the housing marketplace.

Inflation not only increases the overall value of your renovated home each year, it also increases the value of each improvement you've made. This increase in value is the result of the ever-increasing cost of labor and material. Today's brick fireplace valued at about $1,200 will be worth $2,400 in seven years, and buyers will pay for it. At the same time, if you live in the home while inflation works its magic, you can enjoy the greater beauty, space, pride of ownership, and greater function that the improvement provides.

HOUSE STYLE

Style in a home is creating an effect, a feeling, an image. Perhaps it's the beautiful oak mantel over the fieldstone fireplace, or the hardwood floors that give the home a special effect. It could even be the furnishings in which colors and textures blend harmoniously together to capture an aesthetic style.

A house with style is not only pleasing and stimulating to live in, it will also sell faster and get a better price than its unstylish neighbor. Home buyers want style, something special, something out of the ordinary. Buyers want to feel that the house they purchase has a personality, especially after they have saved to make the down payment and committed them-selves to a costly thirty-year mortgage.

The house without style is dull and indefinable. It may be in a good location, solidly constructed and functional, but with-out certain features, it won't be special or unique. The house that lacks style has nothing to distinguish it from all the other houses on the block. It lacks certain features and amenities, has no carefully thought out conveniences—wet bar, fire-place, mirrored walk-in closets, separate laundry room—that make the owners feel distinguished and add a kind of status to their home.

Style is an intangible asset and doesn't necessarily cost a great deal to create. Even a small, inexpensive home can have style. On the other hand, a mansion valued at $1 million can lack definable style. Creating style involves three basic rules: give it a theme, keep it simple, and add features.

Give It a Theme

Giving the house a theme allows you to get a handle on what renovations will enhance or detract from the style you're trying to create. It will also assist you in creating a certain ambience, look, or image for your home.

Let's say, for instance, that your house belongs to a certain style or era, such as Victorian, Tudor, Gothic, or Spanish. If this is the case, then by all means stay with the look that's already been established. You can work wonders accentuating, say, the simplicity of a northeastern Cape Cod or an old mid-western farmhouse. If you own a Victorian or an English Tudor, consider doing some research so you can authenticate the decor. At the same time, you'll want to modernize; how-ever, it's important to retain the antiquity and the nostalgic charm of the original look.

People in today's synthetic culture crave antiquity. They

want to be part of history. They want roots. So by offering them a certain amount of nostalgia, you not only gain by the greater demand for your house, you also get to enjoy these features yourself if you're living there.

If your house does not belong to a noteworthy architectural period, then there are other methods of developing a theme for it. To accomplish this, you have to think clearly about the function of the house. Ask yourself, for whom and for what is the house intended? If it's a family house, how many would be in the family? Is the home for newlyweds or retirees? Is it a second vacation house or a permanent country home? Will it be used for creative work, or will guests be entertained there?

When you carefully think about the function of the house, and about its function for potential buyers, it's easier to conceptualize sensible renovations. The following are examples of how function in a country home can be transposed into style: If the house will be used in winter, you may want to make initial renovations to provide features that keep heating costs down. Think about ease of maintenance, so that if family or guests use the house only on weekends they can keep cleaning to a minimum. And, to most weekend vacationers, luxurious surroundings are less important than serenity and a beautiful view. Elaborate bathrooms or large walk-in closets would not be necessary, but a fireplace or wood-burning stove would be.

Keep It Simple

Keeping it simple is relevant to improvements and to the decor of the house. It means avoiding the overly impressive look that will turn off or disturb potential buyers. This includes excessive or artificial ornamentation, gaudy or distasteful paint on the walls, and bizarre lighting schemes. Such artifice does more to detract from the style of the house than it does to enhance it.

Use authentic materials that will endure. Instead of plastic tile in the bathrooms, use genuine ceramic tile. Instead of synthetic wood flooring, use good cuts of hardwood. And for kitchen and bathroom appliances, install the simplest no-frills models from reputable manufacturers.

Keeping it simple also means maintaining a clean ambience about your house. Visually, the lines of your house and out-buildings—garages, storage shed, pool house—should be kept clean and uncluttered. Store all the unnecessary stuff away, and repair things that are visually disruptive, like a broken antenna or a broken-down tree house. When buyers approach your property, they should be presented with an overall pleasing view, one where the outbuildings and landscaping are in visual harmony with the focal point of the scene, the house.

Add Features

The third rule is to add features that help create style and, inevitably, greater value for your house. Well-conceived amenities will make your home special, unique, more functional than the ordinary house.

Features mean added convenience and function—things you're able to do, feel, or enjoy that you couldn't before the feature was there. Examples are an extra family room with fireplace, an added redwood deck, or a built-in microwave oven. These are all features that owners can enjoy and that add greater value and function to the house.

People want special features and modern conveniences, will look for them, and will pay a premium (more than what the features cost) for the houses that have them. Keep in mind, however, that while some people will pay for an extra bathroom, few will pay for a sauna. Features that are more in demand among buyers add more value to your house than the cost to make them. The following are the special features considered most in demand by contemporary house hunters:

- *Extra room*—One that can be used as a guest bedroom, den, family room, library, or combination of all of these is a real plus.
- *Master suite*—This should be a large bedroom set off from the rest of the house, preferably with its own bath and dressing area. A genuine, first-rate master suite will have such features as a fireplace, sliding glass doors leading to outdoor living areas, and large, mirrored walk-in closets. Buyers are looking for a feeling of warmth and privacy, a kind of combination bedroom and secluded living room.
- *Extra bathroom*—In a house with three bedrooms or more, it's an absolute must. Any family looking to buy a house that requires three bedrooms or more will, no doubt, be grateful for the extra bath. For that reason alone, they will prefer the house that has one over a similar house with no extra bath.
- *Patios and decks*—Extending casual living area to the outdoors not only makes your home more functional, if done properly, it can enhance the visual appeal as well as the value of your home. Be sure to use only weather- and insect-proof materials, while maintaining a pleasing proportion to the house itself. Patios and decks should also be located and landscaped for privacy. A redwood deck, along with a barbecue and clay planters, especially if they overlook a great view, will accentuate any housing plan.

    The more you invest in outdoor amenities, whether they include an enclosed patio or a redwood deck or a brick barbecue, the less likely you'll recoup the investment. Keep your outdoor improvements simple, yet imaginative and practical.

- *Landscaping*—Blossoming plants and special landscaping will enhance the ambience surrounding even the blandest-looking house. Although growing lush gardens may not bring a favorable return on the money and labor invested, it's a helpful feature in the marketing of your home. You need mature landscaping to grace the exterior features of your house. And nothing will lure prospective buyers out of their cars as well as well-kept trees and shrubs and a manicured lawn.

- *Laundry area*—This is a convenience feature appreciated by everyone, especially a large family. If space permits, be sure to provide shelves for laundry supplies and a place to sort and hang large quantities of clothing. You can also use louvered bi-fold doors to conceal the laundry area. Most people like the laundry area to be inside or adjacent to the kitchen. Or the basement is frequently used in order to make use of wasted space and to inexpensively tie in to existing plumbing. For the finishing touch, don't forget adequate lighting.

- *Kitchen conveniences*—Whatever you can add in features that create order and convenience in the kitchen will inevitably pay a bonus. If space permits, the feature of a separate eating area or center work island, especially if it has plenty of storage space, is what buyers want. Buyers are also looking for plenty of storage space in the kitchen. Also consider the natural light-enhancing feature of a skylight. From it you get the extra bonus of the life-giving effect on plants.

PAINTING

Exterior Paint

When considering painting the exterior of the house, be sure to choose the color carefully. The color you select can actually affect the illusion of size. Dark colors will make the house appear small, while light colors make it appear larger. Contrasting trim will always make the house appear smaller. If you're attempting to create a larger look, stay with a single color.

Remember that people in general are conventional. They prefer conventional colors—white, off-white, or tan—over vivid or extraordinary colors. As a rule, the brighter or more unconventional the exterior of the house, the fewer potential buyers will be attracted to it.

Interior Paint

Regarding interior walls, nothing turns off prospective buyers more than dirty, cracked, or water-damaged surfaces. Sometimes all that's necessary to make the walls clean and bright is to wash them. But if your house has been lived in for a while, it's likely you'll need more than tidying up and spackling to patch the holes.

If you have deteriorated plaster, gashes, or large sections of damaged wallboard, the following are a few cost-saving suggestions for wall coverings that will appeal to most prospective buyers.

- Give texture to an uneven wall or ceiling by adding sand to the paint. This will not only hide the flawed unevenness, but will also create an appealing surface.

- Use a less expensive vinyl-coated wallpaper instead of a pure vinyl paper in the kitchen and bathrooms. Apply over it a coat of low-gloss polyurethane, which protects the paper and makes it stain-resistant and scrubbable.
- Cover a badly cracked wall with old barn siding. Assuming that you can locate an old barn and remove the boards with the owner's permission, your only expense will be the cost of transportation, glue, nails, and furring strips.

Like the exterior of the house, the interior walls should be a neutral color in order to appeal to the greatest number of buyers. Tan, beige, and antique white blend with any furniture scheme. Remember that buyers are looking for larger houses. Ultimately, you should make it your objective to have the rooms in your house appear as large as possible. Here are tips on how the use of color will visually enhance the size of rooms:

- Pale, whitish colors reflect light and should be used to make a room appear larger than it is.
- Light-colored ceilings appear higher; dark-colored ceilings appear lower.
- Vertically striped wallpaper visually heightens a room.
- Avoid large or busy prints—wallpapers that have a lot of designs, lines, and contrasting colors. They make a room appear smaller. Wall coverings that have small prints with little contrast make a room seem larger.

CEILINGS AND FLOORS

Uneven, cracked, or stained ceilings detract from what would otherwise be an attractive house. A suspended ceiling can conceal a range of problems, from ceiling sags to unevenness and water damage. You can also texture over the existing damage with a mixture of sand and paint.

Restoring floors to a clean and bright condition is imperative before selling the house. That's because the floor is the first thing most buyers look at when they enter the house. Flooring provides a feeling of solidity, and its color and brightness contribute to visual pleasure and enhance the overall ambience of the house.

Most people prefer hardwood floors to plywood and carpet. If your carpet covers a hardwood floor and is showing signs of wear, consider removing the carpet and restoring the floor. The best way to remove old layers of acrylic or wax is to use elbow grease and number-two steel wool. Wax removers will soften the hardened layers and make the scrubbing easier. Once the layers are removed, apply a coat of polyurethane. It's very durable and virtually maintenance-free; polyurethane doesn't need waxing, and a damp sponge is all that's needed to remove dirt and restore the floor to its original luster.

CREATING NEW LIVING SPACE

Provided the improvements aren't too extravagant, creating new living space will add immediate comfort and value to your home. But before going ahead with major structural changes or adding on, consider certain space-saving improvements that require only minor renovation.

Quite often you can enhance the feeling of space just by storing away paraphernalia. Nooks and crannies or even the space under a stairway can be inexpensively converted to a storage area. Overhead shelves can display knick-knacks around the perimeter of any room. Narrow bookcases can surround a window or frame a fireplace. Narrow shelves on pantry doors and kitchen cabinets can accommodate extra kitchen supplies. These are niceties that buyers fall in love with, especially in the kitchen, where the chef rules the roost. Here are some additional space-saving ideas:

- A center work island with built-in drawers and cabinets in the kitchen
- Built-in drawers under platform beds
- Window seats with storage underneath
- A double-rod clothes rack in high-ceilinged closets
- Multipurpose storage modules that double as room dividers

Structural Alterations

Structural alterations can make better use of existing space in one of three ways: dividing a large room to make small rooms, combining small rooms to create a larger living area, and converting a room to a multipurpose room. Rooms that are often divided are a large bedroom to create two smaller ones, a living room to form a foyer, and a combined living and dining room to form an eat-in breakfast nook and separate living room. Typical conversions include garage to a family room, screened-in patio to den, carport to more kitchen area or den, and deck to enclosed breakfast room.

Structural alterations can be expensive. Nevertheless, when you're providing more usable space, you'll also be adding value to the house. And converting any structure that already has a floor, wall(s), and roof will be less expensive than creating living space from scratch.

Before going ahead with any structural renovation project, carry out certain planning activities. First, picture in your mind how the improvement will look and how much space it will provide. Next, draft a rough floor plan showing door and window locations. Also think about furniture requirements and where you want electrical outlets and light switches. Don't forget to consider how the exterior of the house will be affected. If you're going to convert the carport to a den, try to maintain aesthetic harmony. You want to be consistent with items like windows and doors, keeping them similar in style, size, and height to those in the rest of the house.

Creating more usable space in the basement can be a wise move, provided that the space is properly utilized. Ideas like a workshop, laundry room, or playroom for the kids provide utility to what otherwise would be wasted space. On the other hand, a den, bar, or library wouldn't be that practical or desirable. Most contemporary home buyers prefer living space aboveground, not a gloomy cave below ground level.

Additions

When adding on space, you want to create an economically sound and useful addition to the house. It's imperative that you carefully plan the addition. That's because adding space means spending a large sum of money, not to mention that you or whoever occupies the house will have to live with the addition for a long time.

Start by determining the function of the addition and who will be using it. If you intend to make the addition a family room, consider its primary use. If, for example, teenagers are going to use it to watch television or play loud music in, then you'll want good sound insulation and as much distance as possible from the heart of the house. Conversely, if toddlers use it for a playroom, you'll want it centrally located for easy access.

You also have to plan storage space and the minimum amount of space required for the optimum function of heating, cooling, ventilation, and electrical supply.

Carefully consider design continuity of the addition as it relates to the rest of the house. It's better to extend the style and character of the house to the addition than to add on something that looks out of place. This includes such components as the pitch of the roof and its finish, color of siding, type and location of doors and windows, and wall and floor finishes.

You also have to consider local building code requirements.

Finally, consider such factors as position of the sun and location of neighboring houses in relation to placement of your proposed addition. You don't want to obstruct morning sun from the kitchen or interfere with your privacy, or perhaps that of the neighbors.

IMPROVEMENTS THAT DON'T PAY

There are, of course, certain improvements to the house that don't pay. Home improvements that fail to increase the value of the house typically result from one or more of the following mistakes: overimproving for the neighborhood, poor-quality materials and workmanship, eccentric decor or improvements in a style that is not in harmony with the rest of the house, and availability of a new house of equal size and location for less money than you're asking for yours.

Homeowners too often overimprove. They make inappropriate improvements that might be suitable for them, but not for the overall marketplace. Buyers will pay for an added bathroom, family room, patio, or certain kitchen improvements. But they won't pay for things like tennis courts, sauna baths, or gazebos.

Overimprovement brings to mind two important rules on valuation. They are the *principle of regression* and the *principle of progression*. The principle of regression states that, where properties of unlike quality are placed in the same neighborhood, the worth of the better, higher-quality property is adversely affected and will seek the value level of the lesser properties. In other words, if you build a $100,000 house in a $50,000 neighborhood, the more expensive home will tend to decline in value toward the $50,000 level. The principle of progression states the opposite: if you construct a $50,000 home in a $100,000 neighborhood, the lesser-valued home will increase in value, seeking the level of the higher-quality homes.

Before you consider any improvement, take a close look at other houses in your neighborhood. Ask yourself, Will I be overimproving compared to standards throughout the neighborhood? If all the houses within your tract have two bedrooms and one bath, and you're planning to add on a bath and third bedroom, this would be a mistake. That's because you would be overimproving relative to standards within your vicinity. It would be unlikely that you could raise the price of the house much—surely not enough to recoup what you'll pay for the addition. However, if the other homes in the neighborhood were three-bedroom, two-bath homes, then you could begin your addition confident that when you sell, you'll receive cost plus return on the space you've added.

Also be careful about making improvements in neighborhoods that show signs of decline. You wouldn't want to make costly improvements in the midst of deterioration and devaluation. The potential for making a profit on your improvement should be measured against location, marketing trends, and buyer demand.

Other nonpaying improvements include extravagant items, such as fancy appliances that require a lot of energy and maintenance, and overdone landscaping, such as a ceremonial Buddha or other fancy statues. People want an easy-to-maintain lawn and a few simple shrubs and shade trees, not a botanical jungle that requires huge amounts of labor, water, and expense to maintain. The same holds true for tennis courts, swimming pools, shuffleboard courts, and stucco tree houses. These are luxurious items that certain individuals can't do without. It's highly unlikely the next buyer will find them interesting or be willing to pay for them.

IMPROVEMENTS THAT PAY

More often than not, it's the small improvements that pay the greatest dividends, especially if they're well chosen. Many of these changes are insubstantial relative to labor and materials, yet they do a great deal to create illusions—illusions of roominess, more headroom, more light; illusions that produce a greater feeling of warmth, security, and serenity.

Stylish moldings are a small improvement that not only adds definable style to a plain house, but that also gives traditional charm to the most nondescript rooms. Dating back to the seventeenth century, when New England colonists used it to give their homes distinction, molding today can be purchased in various shapes and sizes. Molding will enhance any room when used to frame archways, decorate around a fireplace, flank doorways and windows, or to create framed panels on paneling or bare walls. It can also be used as chair railing in an old-fashioned kitchen or dining room.

Another small improvement is entryway enhancement. The objective is to impress or captivate potential buyers when they enter the house. First impressions are lasting ones. You can enhance the entryway in a manner that eventually pays big dividends. Sometimes all that's needed is the application of a well-chosen wallpaper, a framed painting, or a stylish framed mirror. Lighting also is important. It should be warm and inviting, not overly bright, especially if you show the house at night.

Another small improvement is porcelain restoration. Stained or chipped porcelain bathtubs, sinks, and appliances reflect lack of proper care and maintenance. If the porcelain surfaces in your house are flawed, they can easily be repaired with porcelain repair paste, available at home improvement centers. Beautiful and stain-free surfaces will most definitely command a premium when it comes time to sell the house.

SUMMARY

When you're thinking of making improvements to the house, especially elaborate ones, ask yourself the following important questions: Does the improvement add space, function, and convenience? Will it look good, or be in harmony with the rest of the house? Are you maintaining a strong theme or style throughout the house? Will the improvements be in tune with what buyers in your area are looking for? And are you overimproving compared to the rest of the neighborhood?

With the exception of the last question on overimproving, all the answers to these questions should be yes. If this is the case, then the chances are very good that you'll make proportionately more, or at least recoup your cost on the improvement, when you sell.

The following are examples of big improvements that are likely to show a proportionate return on investment over a five-year period:

- Energy-efficient fireplace
- Separate master bedroom with bathroom suite
- Walk-in closets with mirrored doors
- Full eat-in kitchen
- Center work island with drawers and cabinets
- Butcher-block counters
- Second bathroom
- Finished laundry area
- Vinyl tile kitchen floor
- Finished hardwood floors
- Bi-fold doors
- Wood decks or a patio done in brick or flagstone

~ 10 ~

Selling Your Property

Unless your real estate investment goals are limited to earning income by renting out your property, you will at some point want to sell your property. Whether you use the services of a Realtor or sell the house yourself and save the commission, keep in mind that, on average, it takes about three months to sell a house. Obviously, then, selling is by no means an easy chore, especially if you intend to get your asking price.

GENERAL GUIDELINES FOR SELLING

If you're in a housing market where properties are in high demand (a seller's market), try to sell the property yourself to avoid paying a Realtor a commission. On the other hand, if you're in an area where there are few buyers (a buyer's market) and many properties, you should hire a Realtor so you can sell your home as quickly and successfully as possible.

Time the offering of your property to coincide with the highest level of market activity. It is best to sell during the spring and fall seasons; that's when most buyers are looking for property (especially if they have children attending school). Avoid trying to sell the property during the winter, particu-

120

larly between Thanksgiving and New Year's Day. During these holiday times, home buyers are usually too preoccupied to take the time necessary to purchase a home.

Price the property right. To arrive at the right price, you can pay $150 or more for an appraisal, or you can study the local market and determine the value yourself. For a quick off-the-cuff evaluation, concentrate on the value per square foot of the comparable properties in your neighborhood. You must first establish the lowest offer you'll accept. Then adjust your price upward from this point. Most buyers like to negotiate, so allow yourself a little flexibility. Price the property reasonably above the lowest you'll accept in order to stimulate bona fide offers.

If you decide to carry a second mortgage or deed of trust when selling the property, be sure to include a "due-on-sale clause" in the document. This clause states that all your remaining equity in the note will be due and payable if the property is ever sold to a person other than the one you are selling to. It will protect you if the property is sold again before you are paid for it. If you decide later that you'd prefer to receive monthly payments after all, you have the option to ignore the clause. But never limit your flexibility by excluding the clause from your note.

Rather than mortgages, use deeds of trust (if available in your state) as the instrument to secure the debt. Mortgages are more cumbersome and take much longer to foreclose on.

Use a neutral third-party escrow agent, usually a title company, to handle all the necessary documents (mortgages and deeds). If the buyer defaults, the escrow agent can return to you all the documents relevant to your property.

If the buyer is to assume your existing loans and is paying your down payment in cash, be sure he or she follows through. Never transfer the title until you are sure the buyer has actually made the down payment and assumed any loans.

You need to put your property, inside and out, in top physical condition. That means thoroughly cleaning not only the living area, but also the exterior grounds, basement, and garage. If necessary, paint the house inside and out. Give special attention to the entryway; it is the first thing prospective buyers will see. (More detailed information about preparing the house for sale is available later in this chapter.)

Avoid the cluttered look by putting excessive furniture in storage. Rearrange and organize what's left to make rooms appear larger. Prospective buyers are looking for spaciousness.

GUIDELINES FOR SELLING THROUGH A REALTOR

Find a real estate agency that advertises aggressively and has many agents or belongs to the multiple-listing service. The more exposure you get, the better.

Be sure you have confidence in the agency you list with.

When you list your home, allow yourself as much flexibility as possible. Never list for extended periods like six months or a year. A three-month listing should be sufficient. If you become dissatisfied with the service you receive from the agency, have the listing agreement rescinded for lack of performance. It isn't necessary to wait out a listing agreement if you feel you're being mistreated.

GUIDELINES FOR SELLING THE
PROPERTY YOURSELF

Never advertise your property address. You want to stimulate interested buyers, not lookers. However, your ads should include the general location and the price. This will eliminate many calls from unqualified buyers. Be sure your headline attracts attention. The heading "For Sale by Owner" always attracts attention. Most buyers automatically figure they can buy at a bargain price because the seller won't be paying a sales commission.

When the prospects begin calling, be prepared. You should know the lot size, age of the house, square feet of living area, names of nearest schools, and major cross streets.

Also be prepared to answer questions about your loan documents and tax information: Is the loan(s) assumable? If so, what is the interest rate? Is there a prepayment penalty? If so, will the lender waive it if the buyer obtains a mortgage from the same lender? What is the current principal balance owing on the loan? How much are the property taxes? Is there a tax and insurance impound account? If so, what is the balance in that account?

In addition, you will need copies of the following documents: the paid tax receipt for the previous year, survey of your property, and evidence of title.

Don't misstate or inflate the facts. You are likely to be tripped up by some unassuming buyer who will refute a false statement instantly. Then the deal is off, for nothing will so undermine the confidence of a buyer as a misstatement knowingly made by one who is attempting to sell real estate.

It's a good idea to put down in writing the features you want to present when making a sale. These may include such things as the view from your property, swimming pool, proximity to shopping, and quality of construction. Writing down these features will help to anchor them in your mind so you can recall them at the proper time.

PREPARING THE PROPERTY BEFORE THE SALE

Whether or not you use the services of a Realtor, you will have to prepare the entire property for its eventual sale. The following material is a guide to preparation in order to get a quick and bona fide offer on your property.

When showing homes to prospective buyers, Realtors often say, "This property has good curb appeal" (i.e., it looks appealing from the curb) or "This house shows well." Their descriptive jargon is relevant to selling your home, because in order to get the best price for your home, you should prepare it to look its best.

Unless you want to sell a fixer-upper or one that looks like a fixer-upper, you have to put the house and the surrounding grounds in order so as to get the most out of the property. Some of the preparation for the sale can simply be tidying up around the exterior of the house. But unless you're an extremely tidy housekeeper, which most of us are not, you'll have to do some minor repairs and touch-ups to meet the standards of good condition. Remember, anything in obvious disrepair will eventually be discounted from the offer price.

First impressions are most important. If the house doesn't look appealing from the curb, the prospective buyer might not consider getting out of the car to look further. The following suggestions will eventually assist in the quick sale of your home and will get the prospect out of the car and into your home for a further inspection.

Exterior

Tidy up all around the exterior grounds by removing any debris, old cars, and so on. Cut the grass, and trim the hedges and shrubs. Organize and neatly arrange items such as outdoor furniture and firewood.

Store away, or have removed from the property, such items as broken-down dishwashers, water heaters, or water softeners. Avoid the look of a junkyard.

Give the lawn a thorough raking. Sweep up the sidewalk and driveway.

Tour the perimeter of your property. Repair any broken fencing, and paint or stain areas that need attention.

Carefully inspect your front door. It's one of the first items your home hunting prospects will examine. If it shows signs of wear, give it a fresh coat of paint or stain. While you're at it, spruce up the house numbers with a touch-up paint job or replace them with new shiny brass ones.

Quite often repainting the entire exterior of the house isn't necessary. Frequently you can substantially improve the appearance of the house simply by repainting the trim.

Repair any broken windows or screens. Then wash them for a brighter appearance.

Interior

When you're finished with the exterior, start on the interior of your home. The objective is to make your home look organized and spacious, bright, warm, and comfortable. I can't emphasize cleanliness enough. Now would be a good time for a thorough cleaning. Remember, a clean house will sell much faster than a dirty one.

Brighten dull rooms with a fresh coat of white, beige, or antique white paint. As I said before, lighter colors make rooms appear bigger and brighter, and neutral colors will go better with the new buyer's furnishings. Instead of taking the time and effort to pull down old wallpaper and put up new, try sprucing up the trim instead.

Cluttered rooms with too much furniture show very poorly. Prospective buyers require lots of room, and that's what they're looking for. So arrange your furniture to make rooms appear more spacious. Put excessive furniture out in storage. De-clutter your home, then rearrange and organize what's left. You'll be surprised how much unwanted stuff can accumulate over the years.

Have a giant garage sale to clear out all your unwanted stuff. You can earn extra money to spend on whatever, and you won't have to pay the movers to relocate all those unwanted items.

Clean all windows and mirrors.

If the carpet is dirty, have it professionally cleaned. If the carpet appears overly worn, consider having it replaced. It is unlikely you will recover the cost of a new carpet in the sale of your home, but the property is likely to sell faster.

In the kitchen, clear off the counters to make your kitchen appear more organized and spacious. Clean and polish all appliances. Finish in the kitchen by making the sink shiny and sparkling.

Clean and shine the tub, toilet, and sink in all the bathrooms.

Break out the toolbox, and start fixing all those little things you've been putting up with all these months—you know, the leaky faucet, loose doorknobs, cracked electrical outlets and switch covers. Secure loose moldings and towel racks and anything that wobbles.

These little items of disrepair can detract from the beauty and function of your home. When a prospective buyer begins examining your home during a walk-through, he or she is mentally keeping track of any shortcomings. Too many little things in disrepair will bring a lower offer—if any at all—than if the house were in excellent condition.

SHOWING YOUR HOME

When it's finally time to show your home to prospective buyers, all the preparations you have made will definitely be worth the effort, as your home will receive more and better offers than if you were ill prepared for the sale. But there are a few additional items you should do just before you show the home that will add that little extra touch of comfort and hominess.

Just before your prospective buyers arrive, clear out the kids and secure the pets where they won't cause any distraction. Turn off the television, and put on some soft music. Turn on all the lights in the house to make it as bright as possible, even during the daytime. If you have a fireplace, fire it up. Liven up the aroma in your home with freshly baked cinnamon rolls right out of the oven. Finish up with clean towels on the racks, and put out some fresh flowers to treat yourself for making your home such a tidy showplace.

When the prospects arrive, make yourself scarce (if using a Realtor, that is). Your absence will make potential buyers more at ease. Your presence will only distract from the job at hand, that of looking over your entire home and answering any questions, which is the agent's responsibility. If you must be there, try to avoid any conversation with the prospects, because the agent needs their full attention to stimulate interest in the features of your home.

Do not complicate the sale of your home by discussing the separate sale of certain appliances or the fact that you wish to keep certain personal items. Personal property, such as furniture and unattached appliances, can be negotiated later, at a more appropriate time.

Always maintain your home in "showplace condition," as you never know when just the right prospect might show up. Your agent will usually make appointments with you for showings. If casual browsers drop in for an unexpected visit, it is best not to show your home. Ask for their name and phone number, and refer the information to your agent.

Keep in mind that it takes time to sell a home. Be patient. Keep your home on the market for as long as it takes. Your home requires adequate exposure to enough prospective buyers for you to consummate a proper sale.

Finally, you might consider offering a one-year home warranty plan, which would offer a little more added value and overcome questions of the working order of major home systems. These policies are available through most national real estate brokerage companies. They protect your buyers for one year against most major repairs.

~ 11 ~
Money-Making Ideas and Tactics

After renovations are complete and the house is in habitable condition, you have to consider what to do with it. Assuming that you'll be investing in another house, moving in, and renovating it, let's consider the options. You could simply rent the original property, sell it for cash, or sell it on installment. Once you've looked over the available options, you can direct your energy to the strategy that will best suit your needs, ability, and long-term goals.

RENTING

If you decide to rent the property, you have to choose either a long-term lease or a month-to-month rental agreement. In most cases, the long-term lease, for one year or more, is better because it limits tenant turnover and assures a stable flow of income over the term.

Simply renting out your property is a proven strategy for realizing a reasonable yield on your investment. However, there's another method that offers tremendous returns and fewer hassles than simply renting out your property. That method is a buy option.

129

Buy Option

A lease with option to purchase, or *buy option*, is a rental agreement where the tenant has the option to purchase the leased property. The buy option is a separate part of the lease that specifies the price and terms of the contract.

For instance, instead of simply renting the house for $700 a month, you could offer the tenant a buy option and collect an additional $200 a month in option fees. The additional $200 is applied toward the down payment or purchase price. This way you'd receive an extra $200 monthly.

The buy option strategy can be a lucrative tool in realty investing. It has a broad market because many potential home buyers like the idea of making their down payment on the installment plan. Aside from being more profitable, the buy option has a number of other advantages over renting:

- Buy option tenants take better care of the premises. That's because they tend to make improvements to it, planning to own it some day.
- You save a sales commission because you don't have to find a buyer. That's a savings of about $6,000 on a $100,000 sale!
- If the tenant fails to exercise the option, he or she forfeits all option fees already paid.

Please note that it's better if the existing financing on the property is assumable. Otherwise, the tenant will have to obtain new financing when the option is exercised.

Installment Sale

Instead of renting your property to a tenant, you can sell it on installment. Let's say, for example, you purchased a property for $60,000 with an existing assumable loan at 9 percent. You also had the seller carry back a mortgage that's assumable at 9 percent. After fixing up the property, you determine that you can sell it for $80,000 with $8,000 down. In doing so, you could allow the buyer to assume all this built-in financing. But why not make a profit on the financing and create a new all-inclusive mortgage?

You could, for example, offer the buyer a new all-inclusive mortgage for the $72,000, owing at 10.5 interest for 20 years. This way you make a profit in the spread in interest rates. You continue paying on the existing 9 percent loans, while the buyer pays you 10.5 interest on the new loan.

Sale for Cash

You also have the option of selling the property outright for all cash; the buyer must originate a new loan in order to cash you out. Being totally cashed out of the property means, of course, that you don't bear the risk of the buyer's defaulting, as with the installment sale. The other advantage is that you immediately realize the gain after the sale, which means you'll have plenty of cash on hand. But, this is an advantage only if you have a good place to reinvest the proceeds.

Now consider the disadvantages. The most undesirable aspect of such a sale is that now you have to find another investment for the proceeds from the sale. Good realty investments are not only hard to find, but are very time-consuming as well. You could put the proceeds in savings, but who wants to earn a meager pretax yield of 5 percent? Realistically, if you plan to build a multiproperty estate, you have to seek out another property to invest in—one that can earn more than a meager 5 percent and that can shelter the gains earned on the property sold.

The other glaring disadvantage of being cashed out is that, under certain conditions, you have to pay income taxes on the gain from the sale. If you are selling your principal residence, however, you can defer payment of income taxes if, within a year of the sale, you buy another property of equal or greater value.

HOW TO BUILD A MULTIPROPERTY ESTATE

Creating a portfolio of several properties is the systematic process of continual investment in more properties, using the earnings and equities of the property already acquired. The foundation of your multiproperty portfolio will likely be the home you already own or are planning to buy.

You might be a little skeptical at first, especially if you haven't already experienced the satisfaction and profitability that ownership of real property offers. You might say to yourself, "There's no way that I can convert a small amount of savings into a massive portfolio of property that I can quit my job and retire on." Believe me . . . you can do it! You just need to be methodical and patient, letting time and appreciation work for you. You need to persevere and apply the strategies and guidelines set forth in this book.

The Estate-Building Process

There are three key factors to the estate-building process. They are price appreciation, tax reduction ability, and refinancing benefit.

Price Appreciation

Inflation and demand for a limited supply of land lead to appreciation in the price of real estate. Depending on how strong the market is in your city, you can expect an annual rate of appreciation of about 6 to 10 percent. Your equity in the home also grows each year as the result of mortgage paydown.

Not only is inflation on your side as a realty investor, but time is also. As time passes, rents on income property can be increased. This means that the first property you purchased years ago, which generated little or no income then, can eventually develop positive cash flow from these increases. Today a multitude of owners live very comfortably off the income generated from their properties. They live by a rule that states, Buy all the income property you can when you're young, then enjoy the income benefits when you're old.

Tax Reduction Ability

Besides the benefits of appreciation, property owners enjoy the advantage of having more spendable income because they can reduce their income taxes. Homeowners are allowed deductions for mortgage interest, interest on home equity loans, and property taxes. In addition, they can defer paying tax on gains indefinitely when selling or trading the property.

Owners of income property can deduct a depreciation allowance and certain expenses. If you combine all these tax shelter benefits, most owners of income property can show a taxable loss on their tax return, even when their cash flow is positive.

Refinancing Benefit

The refinancing benefit evolves over time as the property continues to appreciate. Once the equity has grown by a worthwhile amount, say, 40 percent or more, you can borrow against it to make additional investments. The result will be maximum use of leverage, or showing a greater return on your investment by using other people's money.

Investing in a Second House

After years of price appreciation and mortgage paydown on your primary residence, it's time to think about investing in a second house. If you have finished with the renovations and have the required capital to invest in a second house, by all means do so.

Assuming that all renovations have been completed and you have enough funds, after investing in a second house you have two options. You can stay in the primary residence and rent the second house to tenants, or you can move into the second house and rent out what was your primary residence.

I recommend the latter of the alternatives. Experience has taught me that it's much simpler and less expensive, even with the inconvenience of moving every time another house is purchased.

During a certain period in my investment career, I was purchasing a house about every six months. I'd buy a house, move into it, spend half a year renovating it, then I wouldn't rent it to tenants until I had saved enough money and had bought another house to move into. This way I had prospects coming to my door, instead of meeting them at the other property. And it was efficient, because I made renovations while living in the property, instead of continually transporting supplies over to the other property to work on it.

About the only meaningful disadvantage of operating this way is that you have to move the household belongings every time you buy another house. However, the inconvenience is overshadowed by the convenience of renovating the house while living in it. You won't have to constantly drive to the other property in order to make renovations or to show it to rental prospects. Furthermore, the house you're living in will show better than the unfurnished and unlived-in second house.

Creating a multiproperty estate doesn't just happen overnight. You begin with the first property. Add to that some sweat equity and time to help increase its value. Before you know it, a few years have passed by and your home has substantially increased in value. Then you can either borrow against the equity or save a down payment in order to buy a second house. After that, you can start thinking about a third house, and so on.

The Plan in Action

Consider putting yourself in the following scenario that involves subsequent investments in several houses over the next twenty years. Today, in year one, you buy an undervalued fixer-upper and move into it. You occupy that house for the next three years while making renovations that increase its value. You also start saving money for a second property. You will buy it when you have saved enough funds and completed the renovations on your residence.

Beginning in year four, you buy a second house with accumulated savings. You rent the primary residence to tenants, then move into the second house and renovate it.

About three years later, in year seven, you buy house number three. It could be purchased with accumulated savings or by refinancing house number one, since its value has likely doubled in seven years. Then you rent house number two, and you move into house number three and renovate it.

During the next thirteen years, you continue the process of buying, renovating, and renting properties. At the end of twenty years, and depending on your aggressiveness as an investor and your selection of properties, you should be able to generate enough income to comfortably retire on your multiproperty estate!

THRIVING IN A CYCLICAL MARKET

Recession, depression, buyer's market, seller's market, hyper-inflation—real estate markets are cyclical. Property values fluctuate depending on overall economic conditions. Nevertheless, over the long term, virtually every well-located property endures these up-and-down swings and appreciates in value. Inflation accounts for some of this increase in value, but another contributing factor is real estate's unique characteristic of increasing demand caused by population growth, coupled with a finite supply (they just aren't making any more land).

It's relatively easy for most realty investors to prosper in strong, thriving markets. But being able to endure and make a profit during depressed markets is what separates the winners from the losers. Thriving in a depressed real estate market usually means having staying power—in other words, not being forced to sell. This also means maintaining your job, not being laid off, while your neighbors go unemployed. The only time you really want to sell is when you choose to do so, not when you're forced to sell because you need the money.

So, if you can stay liquid (keep emergency cash on hand) during the hard times, you can usually survive. Meanwhile, all your neighbors who overextended themselves and are forced to sell will have to take much less for their properties when they do sell in a depressed market.

SOME FINAL WORDS OF ADVICE

Most of the labor involved in buying distressed real estate falls into the following areas: arranging financing, making renovations, and managing the investment. But these activities don't have to be laborious; in fact, besides being very profitable, real estate investment can actually be fun and exciting. This is especially true if you enter a joint venture with someone who shares your interests and can complement your particular skills and abilities. This way you not only share the work, but you also share the risk and the profits.

The idea is to find someone who can work within the partnership to complement your abilities. For instance, if you are skilled at managing—doing things like bookkeeping and renting apartments, then take on a partner who can do renovations and maintenance.

Finally, when it comes to profitable investment in distressed real estate, you should be very knowledgeable and selective. Like some crude gems, with a little polish a select few of these diamonds in the rough often become sparkling jewels. Yet regardless of the effort or amount of polish applied by the prospector, the majority of his or her finds are mere industrial diamonds and will never be worth more than the cost to acquire them. Your skill is what will identify the properties with the potential to sparkle.

Index